GREATEST
NATIONAL PARKS

GREATEST
NATIONAL PARKS
OF THE WORLD

AARON MILLAR

Published in the UK in 2018 by
Icon Books Ltd, Omnibus Business Centre,
39–41 North Road, London N7 9DP
email: info@iconbooks.com
www.iconbooks.com

Sold in the UK, Europe and Asia
by Faber & Faber Ltd, Bloomsbury House,
74–77 Great Russell Street,
London WC1B 3DA or their agents

Distributed in the UK, Europe and Asia
by Grantham Book Services, Trent Road,
Grantham NG31 7XQ

Distributed in Australia and New Zealand
by Allen & Unwin Pty Ltd,
PO Box 8500, 83 Alexander Street,
Crows Nest, NSW 2065

Distributed in South Africa by
Jonathan Ball, Office B4, The District,
41 Sir Lowry Road, Woodstock 7925

Distributed in India by Penguin Books India,
7th Floor, Infinity Tower – C, DLF Cyber City,
Gurgaon 122002, Haryana

Distributed in Canada by Publishers Group Canada,
76 Stafford Street, Unit 300, Toronto, Ontario M6J 2S1

Distributed in the USA by Publishers Group West,
1700 Fourth Street, Berkeley, CA 94710

ISBN: 978-178578-339-5

Images – see individual pictures

Typeset and designed by Simmons Pugh

Printed and bound in the UK by Clays Ltd, St Ives plc

For my children, Cameron and Elise
'This I'll Defend'

ABOUT THE AUTHOR

Aaron Millar is an award-winning travel writer. He contributes regularly to *The Times*, the *Observer*, *National Geographic Traveller* and many other national and international publications. He has presented travel documentaries for National Geographic and is the 2014 and 2017 British Guild of Travel Writers Travel Writer of the Year, the 2014, 2016 and 2017 winner of the Visit USA Best National Newspaper Feature Award and the winner of the 2017 IPW Best Destination Travel Feature Award. He grew up in Brighton, England and at the time of writing is hiding out in the Rocky Mountains of Boulder, Colorado.

For more about Aaron, visit: www.thebluedotperspective. com, @AaronMWriter

'Aaron Millar has a great way with words and knows how to bring a place and story to life. A pleasure to read.'
Jane Dunford, Travel Editor, *Guardian*

'Aaron Millar's travel writing is, quite simply, among the best there is. Both lyrical and informative, it is a joy to read.'
Jane Knight, Travel Editor, *The Times*

'Aaron Millar's travel writing is always inspiring, insightful and compelling. This book is a fascinating read and will make you want to get up and see the world.'
Pat Riddell, Editor, *National Geographic Traveller* (UK)

CONTENTS

Europe

Africa

Asia

Oceania

INTRODUCTION

John Muir, the great environmentalist, said: 'Going to the mountains is going home.' The wilderness isn't a luxury; it isn't a pretty postcard or a quick photograph from a car window screen. It's an essential part of who we are. Ninety nine per cent of the evolution of humankind has been spent intimately connected with the outdoors. Only in the last 10,000 years have we turned to settlements and cultivated land, and only in the last few hundred have those spiralled into the metropolises we see today.

You may spend your days in front of a computer screen, you may live in a city, or have never stood on a mountain summit or seen the true glory of the stars at night, but make no mistake: the wilderness is inside of you. If this book aspires to an idea it is this: love your world, live life to the full and feed your wildness well.

The first national park, Yellowstone, was established in 1872. It was an era of human domination over nature, and so the idea that wild lands should be set aside for conservation was a radical one. But it spread. According to the International Union for Conservation of Nature there are over 100,000 national parks and similar protected reserves in the world today, covering roughly 12 per cent of the Earth's surface. They provide economic benefits, helping to support local communities and indigenous populations; they protect the world's key biodiversity hot spots and threatened species; they preserve our history and culture;

they offer opportunities for scientific research and have proven vital in breakthroughs in medicine, climate change and more. Perhaps, most importantly though, they protect the land itself: national parks are the guardians of wonder, the last bastions of the most beautiful places on Earth.

And they're ours. Reserves can be private property; national parks are, by definition, owned by us. They represent the identity of a country, the soul of a people. When we look across the red rock spires of the Grand Canyon, we connect with the spirit of the American West. When we walk among the endless grasslands of the Serengeti, we walk with the Maasai people too. National parks do not just show us a place, they let us feel it. They are the epitome of travel dreams, the canvas for the greatest adventures of your life.

I want to take you on an adventure too. Through the pages of this book, I hope to make the world's most spectacular landscapes come alive. I want you to feel what it's like to look a grizzly in the eye in the backcountry of Denali, to explore lost cities in the Amazon and share airig liquor with the golden eagle hunters of the Mongolian steppe. This isn't just a guidebook, a list of sights to see and things to do; it's a window into the most awe-inspiring experiences on the planet.

Some of the national parks are well known, but many have never been featured in a major compendium before: North Luangwa, in Zambia, home of the walking safari, visited by only 500 people a year; Madidi, in Bolivia, one of the most bio-diverse place on the planet; Gwaii Haanas, in British Columbia, the Galápagos of the North. At the end of every chapter, I'll provide the insider information, and expert tips, on how to see them best, from catching a 'superbloom' of wildflowers in Death Valley to having the ancient Mayan ruins of Tikal all to yourself, as well as recommendations for what else to see while you're there, helping you to turn that one national park into a bucket list trip of a lifetime.

That's important, because the more we disconnect from the natural world, the more we need it. Wilderness experiences have been shown to have a huge range of health benefits, from reducing stress and anxiety to boosting self-esteem, creativity, confidence and even helping people with depression and PTSD. Human beings have evolved for life on the savannah but we spend it on social media feeds. Modern life, that relentless drive for success when every second is filled with information, when the stars are replaced with TVs and the natural world is seen only through computer screens, has swelled our egos and diminished our soul.

That's why national parks are so vital. They're also how we save the planet, because the first step in conservation is to fall in love with the outdoors: climb a mountain, jump in a river, immerse yourself in wonder. The rest will follow. '[In] wildness,' John Muir said, 'lies the hope of the world.' At a time when we are bombarded with bad news, when there are people in power who still view nature as a thing to exploit, a means to profit, rather than a living system with intrinsic rights, national parks are a rare beacon of light. Nature is our home. Feed your wildness well.

NORTH AMERICA

YELLOWSTONE NATIONAL PARK, WYOMING, MONTANA AND IDAHO

The American painter Anne Coe called Yellowstone 'the place where the centre of the Earth finds an exit and gives us a glimpse of its soul.' Bubbling hot springs and super-heated geysers explode hundreds of feet into the air; the ground shakes and hisses; there are boiling pools of pure sapphire and thermal jets etched in rainbows of red, yellow and green. Yellowstone is fire and violence, a primeval landscape unlike anywhere else on Earth.

Established in 1872, it is also the world's first national park and the start of a conservation movement that has now spread to thousands of protected areas around the globe. Europeans discovered it through fur trappers and mountain men, who travelled into the vast reaches of the American wilderness in the early 19th century in search of beaver pelts and furs to trade. They returned with tall tales of a magical landscape where the Earth boiled and jets of scalding water exploded from the ground. Expeditions followed: the Folsom–Cook trip of 1869, the first organised exploration of the region, called it a 'masterpiece of nature's handiwork'; and the Hayden expedition of 1871, who returned with photographs and drawings that convinced Congress to sign its protection into law.

Today it is home to the largest active geyser basin on the planet: some 10,000 hydrothermal features, the highest concentration

Photo: Aaron Zhu

on earth, including close to 500 individual geysers, roughly half the world's total. Old Faithful is the star, a giant plume of white water that explodes up to 180 feet in the air. But its fame rests on its reliability, erupting like clockwork every 90 minutes or so. Giant Geyser is bigger, reaching 250 feet, but hard to predict; Steamboat Geyser holds the world record for the tallest on Earth, but you may wait 50 years to see it.

The real wonder of Yellowstone, however, is not one single feature, but the basin as a whole. There are geysers shaped like castle turrets, others like beehives or fountains, even one that looks like a lion's head, steam pouring out as it roars. Some scream suddenly, like rockets shooting in the air, others build slowly, bubbling like a witch's brew. There are mud pots the colour of cinnamon and scalding pools edged in slicks of amber and green, like a watercolour painting.

Nearby to the main geyser basin is the Grand Prismatic Spring, the largest hot spring in the United States at 370 feet across, ringed in rainbows of orange, yellow and green, with bright turquoise water in the centre, like the blue eye of a giant peering up from the bowels of the Earth. Fifty miles away, in the far north of the park, are the Mammoth Hot Springs: natural travertine sculptures formed from mineral-rich water pumped up through cracks in the Earth that solidify into ever-changing forms, dripping down the hillside like an enormous abstract art installation.

The aesthetics are spectacular, but what's truly mind-blowing is that each of these thermal features are alive. Microscopic bacteria and algae, called thermophiles, exist in these extreme conditions, creating vibrant strips of colour as they feed in distinct bands of heat – blue for archaea, which lives at 199 degrees Fahrenheit; yellow for bacteria at 166 degrees Fahrenheit; green, algae at 140 degrees Fahrenheit; orange, protozoa at 133 degrees Fahrenheit. They are among the least understood organisms on Earth, but they are involved with some of the most cutting-edge science of our time, including breakthroughs in DNA sequencing and the fight against AIDS, Ebola and other diseases. They're even involved in the search for extraterrestrial life. By comparing the fossil records of thermophiles found in the park with rocks brought back from Mars, NASA is hoping to one day prove definitively that we are not alone – far from little green men, it turns out that the aliens may look a lot like the geyser basin of Yellowstone National Park.

But there's another experiment happening here too and, arguably, it's the most important of all. At the turn of the 20th century wolves had been hunted to near extinction across the United States. In Yellowstone, the last one was killed in 1926. But now they're back, having been reintroduced to the park in 1995, and the effect they're having is nothing short of miraculous.

The problem was the elk. Without their top predator, they had run riot, reducing the vegetation, in many areas, to wasteland. This had a knock-on effect across the entire ecosystem, suppressing the growth of forests, plant-life and destroying key habitats. The thought was that humans could intervene and cull the herds to manageable levels. But despite their best efforts, Yellowstone was slowly dying.

When the wolves were reintroduced, just 41 in total, the effect was immediate. They killed some elk, of course, but more importantly they changed the behaviour of the herds – something that humans simply couldn't do. The elk stopped grazing in places they knew they would be vulnerable. As they did so, those places immediately started to flourish again: barren valleys became forests, songbirds returned, the rivers thrived with fish and beaver. In the ecological blink of an eye the entire ecosystem was transformed.

It is, perhaps, the most striking example we have of a concept called 'rewilding' and it's revolutionizing how we approach conservation around the world. Rather than maintain an ecosystem through human intervention, the wolves of Yellowstone remind us to just let go.

That's what makes Yellowstone great: it is more than a window into the inner workings of the world, more than a glimpse of the Earth's soul; it is, perhaps, a spark of hope too, a landscape as wild as the wolves; a primeval world unlike anywhere else on Earth.

WHERE: Wyoming, Montana and Idaho. There are numerous gateway towns, depending on where you're coming from. See website for details: *www.nps.gov/grte*

DON'T MISS: The Boiling River. Close to the Mammoth Hot Springs, near the north entrance, is the most extreme natural hot tub in the world: underground springs pipe steaming hot mineral-rich water directly into the Yellowstone River, creating warm eddies surrounded on all sides by freezing rapids and icy flow.

TOP TIP: Avoid the crowds of summer and come in May for calving season; September and October for the elk rut; or December to February to have the magic of the thermal world all to yourself.

WHILE YOU'RE THERE: Grand Teton National Park is just a few miles south of Yellowstone and home to the 'mountains of the imagination' as they're known locally – one of the most photogenic ranges in the world, as well as pristine alpine lakes, magnificent wildlife and over 200 miles of hiking trails: *www.nps.gov/grte*

YOSEMITE NATIONAL PARK, CALIFORNIA

In 1903, President Roosevelt spent three days camping in the backcountry of Yosemite, with the legendary naturalist and environmental campaigner, John Muir. He described the experience as '... like lying in a great solemn cathedral, far vaster and more beautiful than any built by the hand of man.' Yosemite has that effect on you. There is something intangible, almost spiritual, in the harmony of natural elements, as if the Earth here, among the smooth granite peaks of the High Sierra, the lush pine forests and waterfalls that plummet thousands of feet to the valley floor, had finally carved its masterpiece, the perfect balance of colour, light and form.

It is not the first national park (that honour belongs to Yellowstone), but it is, arguably, more fundamental. Yosemite is the first protected wilderness area in the country, signed into law in 1864 by President Abraham Lincoln. Up until that point the wilderness was seen solely as a resource for human exploitation. That wild lands should remain untouched and not subject to the dominion of man was a revolutionary concept. But it spread. Today, Yosemite is widely credited with inspiring America's national park movement, which has since expanded to thousands of protected parks and reserves around the globe.

One man in particular is to thank. John Muir first visited Yosemite in 1868, at the age of 30, returning the next year to work as a ranch hand and then a shepherd's assistant, guiding a flock of 2,000 sheep through the foothills of the Sierra Nevada Mountains. It was an experience that changed him fundamentally. A deeply religious man, he found in the

Photo: chenshyuan

rocks and streams of Yosemite a connection to God that was more profound than any he had experienced before. Being in nature, for Muir, became akin to communing with the divine. 'In God's wildness lies the hope of the world,' he wrote. 'No temple made with hands can compare with Yosemite.'

He would spend the rest of his life campaigning for the protection of Yosemite, and other wild lands, and was instrumental in establishing it as a national park. Muir envisioned a place where 'thousands of tired, nerve-shaken, over-civilised people [would begin to find out] that going to the mountains is going home; that wildness is a necessity.' And that's exactly what Yosemite has become: a sanctuary, an escape, a cathedral of light and stone.

There are many highlights. Yosemite Valley is the central hub, 'a glitter of green and golden wonder', as the great photographer Ansel Adams, who made his name photographing these landscapes, described it. On the north side of the valley is El Capitan, a 3,000-foot vertical face that has taunted and mesmerised the world's greatest climbers for over 50 years. In the far west is the cracked edifice of Half Dome, one of the most iconic peaks on the planet, and Glacier Point, one of the most spectacular views in the country, the sparkling granite of the high country rolling endlessly to the horizon.

Then there are the waterfalls. Niagara may be the country's largest by volume, but Yosemite Falls is thirteen times as tall, a magnificent series of three cascades that plummet 2,425 feet from the high country to the valley floor – almost twice the height of the Empire State Building in total. Nearby is Ribbon Falls, the longest single vertical drop in North America at 1,600 feet, covering the ground in misty rainbows and the thunder of its crash; and Sentinel Falls, a 2,000-foot silver ribbon of snow-melt, like an enormous waterslide. But, perhaps most special of all is Horsetail Falls, in the north of the valley. For most of the year, it's nothing more than a trickle but in late February the last embers of the setting sun reflect off its water, transforming the cascade into a river of falling fire – one of the most unique natural phenomena in the country.

But the real magic of Yosemite is in the backcountry. It is thought that 95 per cent of visitors cram themselves into less than 5 per cent of the park – and most will never hike further than a mile from their car. But away from those crowds there is a wilderness filled with nothing but silence and the glittering vastness of the mountains. Out here, it's still possible to find something of that connection Muir held so dear, in the wildflowers that spring from lightning-burnt forests, the granite peaks that rise from the valley like giant stone totems, the glacier lakes that reflect the sunrise in mirror perfection.

John Muir said: 'There is a love of wild nature in everybody, an ancient mother-love ever showing itself whether recognised or no, and however covered by cares and duties.' Yosemite washes those cares away. Here, in this vast cathedral of stone, this masterpiece of light and form, we are reminded that nature is not a thing outside of us, but an essential part within. Wildness is not a luxury, it's a necessity. Like Muir said: 'going to the mountains is going home.'

WHERE: Mariposa County, California, four hours west of San Francisco. There are numerous gateway towns, depending on where you enter. See website for further details: *www.nps.gov/yose*

DON'T MISS: The High Sierra Loop: A spectacular 49-mile

backcountry trail that traverses many of the same paths that John Muir walked his first summer in the Sierras. The trail is interspersed by five historic camps, each about ten miles apart, offering proper beds, heated cabins and home-cooked meals – the business class of backpacking. But it's popular – accommodation is provided on a lottery basis. Apply early: *www.yosemitepark.com/high-sierra-camp-how-to-apply.aspx*

TOP TIP: Come in May and June to see the waterfalls at their most spectacular. Lake Tenaya, in the north of the park, near Tuolumne Meadows, is the best lake for swimming and has one of America's most beautiful, and undiscovered, beaches.

WHILE YOU'RE THERE: Visit Sequoia and Kings Canyon National Park, three hours south – home of General Sherman, the 2.7-million-pound, 275-foot-tall largest tree on Earth: *www.nps.gov/seki*

GRAND CANYON NATIONAL PARK, ARIZONA

Two hundred and seventy seven miles long, eighteen miles wide at its peak and with up to 6,000 feet from its tip to the valley floor, the Grand Canyon may not be the largest canyon in the world – Peru's Colca Canyon is almost twice as deep and Tibet's Yarlung Zangbo Grand Canyon is 35 miles longer and 12,000 feet taller – but it is, surely, the most spectacular: a kaleidoscopic gorge of the Colorado River filled with amber spires, golden buttes and sheer red rock cliffs that glow at sunset like embers from a fire. The poet Harriet Monroe called it 'the abode of gods', and so it is. A land too humbling to be real; on a clear day you can see for a hundred miles and still only take a fraction in.

But aesthetics are only part of it. The real wonder of the Grand Canyon are the rocks themselves. The Colorado River began carving into the Colorado Plateau, a 140,000-square-mile section of exposed Earth's crust in the Four Corners region of Utah, Arizona, New Mexico and Colorado, about 6 million years ago. As it descended, it gathered speed and force, flowing as fast as 300,000 cubic feet per second, digging into the plain and scouring the gorge ever deeper.

What it revealed is astonishing. The further down it cut, the older the rocks were that it exposed: from the 260-million-year-old Kaibab Limestone at its summit to the 1.8-billion-year-old Vishnu Schist at the river's edge today. In total, a staggering 32 per cent of the Earth's entire natural history is written into the sheer cliffs of the Grand Canyon. It is the most complete geologic record on the planet – showing everything from the first life forms, through the evolution of plants, fish and amphibians to mammals. Being here is like looking at a tapestry of the past etched into stone: layer upon layer, we see oceans rise and fall, swamps become desert, mountains tumble and lift again. It is, perhaps, the most startling example on Earth of what geologists call 'deep time' – the unimaginable lifespan of the planet, a longevity that is simply too vast for human minds to fully comprehend.

But the rocks are just the start. Within the canyon walls there are waterfalls and sandy beaches, emerald pools and hanging gardens of honey mesquite and coyote willow. Bison, elk and bighorn sheep roam free; one of the rarest birds in the world, the California condor, makes its home here; peregrine falcons, the fastest, race on thermals above. In total, the canyon supports five of the seven North American life zones – a snapshot of the entire continent stepped into distinct bands of elevation from low, hot deserts through forests of ponderosa pine to rich meadows of Aspen and Douglas fir.

There's history too. Native Americans have been living here, or migrating through, for thousands of years, including the Hualapai and the Havasupai tribes who still reside on ancestral lands in and around the canyon today. Our hiking trails are formed from their hunting paths; their petroglyphs still colour the chasm walls; there are ancient food stores cut high into the cliffs and caves where sacred 2,000-year-old split-twig-figurines have been placed ceremoniously within.

There is much else to see too. The South Rim is the most popular destination, with iconic viewpoints such as Hopi and Mather Point, but it's crowded, receiving 90 per cent of the park's close to 6 million annual visitors. For a quieter, and wilder, experience head to the remote North Rim, where the views are just as jaw-dropping but the crowds a fraction as thin. Don't miss the chance to explore the base of the canyon too: mule trips or hikes offer the best opportunity to see the geology of the rocks up close, as well as much of the park's history.

But make time to explore the canyon outside the park boundaries too. For many, a float trip down the Colorado River, whether half a day or as much as two weeks on the water, is one of the great American adventures, emulating the journey of John Wesley Powell who spent three months rafting through the canyon in 1869, filling in one of the last blank spots on the American map. Just as impressive is a visit to the Havasupai reservation, where camping and lodge accommodation is offered in the remote Supai village, at the base of the canyon. Surrounded by groves of giant cottonwoods, the turquoise waters of Havasu Creek and three spectacular waterfalls tumbling down the red rocks cliffs all around, it's widely considered to be one of the most beautiful campgrounds in America.

But whatever you do, it will be that view, those golden canyon walls and endless amber spires that will stay with you forever. The author J.B. Priestly said that the Grand Canyon was: 'not a show place [or] a beauty spot, but a revelation'. He was right. This is nature at its most unfathomably large. To see those cliffs, sullen in the pink silence of dawn; angry in thunder; shifting with the moods of the day, is to peer into the bones of the Earth itself, to see its story etched in stone and grasp, in an instant, the impermanence of all things; the flash of our own lives and, yet, the wonder to which we also bear witness.

WHERE: North-west Arizona, 80 miles north of Flagstaff. The nearest town for the South Rim is Tusayan: *www.nps.gov/grca*

DON'T MISS: Hopi Point, on the South Rim, is one of the best places to watch the sunset, but it can get crowded in the summer. Head to Yaki or Pima Points instead for a quieter view – a Park Ranger favourite. Point Imperial, on the North Rim, is one of the best places in the park to watch the sunrise.

TOP TIP: Accommodation in the canyon, and at the Havasupai reservation (*www.theofficialhavasupaitribe.com*), gets booked up months in advance – but is also the highlight of many trips. Plan ahead and book your accommodation at least a year in advance to avoid disappointment. Hiking in summer can be unbearably hot – come spring or autumn for a better and safer experience.

WHILE YOU'RE THERE: Visit Monument Valley Navajo

Photo: National Park Service Digital Image Archives

Tribal Park, 150 miles to the north-east – an otherworldly landscape of red rock buttes rising from the desert like giant fists punching up from under the Earth. A sacred place to the Navajo it is also a famous film location for many of the world's greatest westerns, including *Stagecoach* and *The Searchers* among many others: *www.navajonationalparks.org/ navajo-tribal-parks/monument-valley-navajo-tribal-park*

DENALI NATIONAL PARK AND PRESERVE, ALASKA

Denali is unique among America's national parks. Most are managed for human recreation: there are roads, hiking trails, viewpoints – threads of order woven into the wilderness like geometric lines on a splash of paint. Denali is different; it's raw and unkempt, as wild as Alaska itself. In over 9,000 square miles of wilderness, there is only one sliver of road, just 92 miles long – the faintest of pencil lines on a canvas as big as your house. The rest is completely untouched. Cars are not allowed; there are no trails bar a handful that hug the entrance and a few spots along the road. To really see it you must travel as the animals do, fording rivers, climbing steep crags and rocky scree, treading carefully on glacier ice. This is the far north of America, the real backcountry. You come here to disappear, to feel the rhythm of the seasons, the silence of winter, the endless light of summer. In a world where civilisation creeps ever forward, Denali is the ultimate escape.

At its centre is the mountain. Rising 20,310 feet from sea level, Denali (formerly known as Mount McKinley), which means 'The Great One' or 'The High One' in native

Athabascan, is the tallest peak in North America and the third biggest of the Seven Summits – the highest mountains on each of the seven continents. Counting only the vertical rise, which is measured from its base to the summit, rather than its height from sea level, Denali is 18,000 feet tall – 6,000 feet taller than Mount Everest – the greatest vertical rise of any mountain on Earth above sea level.

It's one of the most dangerous mountains on Earth too. The upper half is permanently covered in snow and glaciers, some wider than 30 miles across. In winter temperatures can reach minus 75 degrees Fahrenheit; gusts of wind race past at 200 miles per hour; outside of Antarctica the summit of Denali is the coldest place on the planet. Yet, hundreds of people still climb it each year. In summer, a mere 40 per cent of those that attempt it will stand upon its peak; in winter only a handful have ever succeeded, and many die trying each year.

But The Great One is only part of the reason people come. For most, it's the wildlife. In a single day, it's possible to see all of Denali's Big Five – the top mammals that live in the park year round: caribou, moose, Dall sheep, wolves and grizzly bears. But that's just the start: black bears, lynx and red fox race across the tundra; golden eagles circle above. The wide-open, mostly treeless landscape of Denali makes sightings relatively easy, with the best opportunities usually coming from on-board one of the park's elevated tour buses, which traverse the solitary road throughout the summer. It's an inspiring experience and, undoubtedly, one of the best opportunities in the country for viewing a huge range of wildlife in close proximity. But for the intrepid, it's just the beginning.

The true soul of Denali is beyond the safety of the road, in the wild tundra and taiga forests, in the icy peaks and rapids filled with salmon. The Athabascan people have lived

here for thousands of years, hunting in the lowland hills, fishing the rivers, gathering blueberries by the side of lakes each spring – many still live here today, practising that same subsistence existence, keeping their culture and knowledge alive for each new generation.

When you leave that ribbon of road, when you walk into the backcountry and search for that wild existential adventure, that solitude and danger away from the comforts of civilisation, you live as they once did. It is challenging and remote, an untrammelled land of mystery and unbounded exploration that requires resilience, endurance and courage. But the rewards are great. For here, in the silence of the true wilderness, we can listen to the original heartbeat of the country and, if we're lucky, we can hear ourselves also in the echo it returns.

WHERE: Southern central Alaska, 240 miles north of Anchorage. The nearest towns are Nenana Canyon and Healy: *www.nps.gov/dena*

DON'T MISS: The Northern Lights. Winter offers the best chances of seeing the Aurora, but they are often visible as early as September. Check the University of Alaska Fairbanks' website for predictions of solar activity: an indicator of likely sightings, then time your visit with a cloudless, moonless night of the brightest displays: *www.gi.alaska.edu/AuroraForecast*

TOP TIP: Enter the annual 'Road Lottery' for the chance to drive your own car the full length of the park road on specified dates each September, spotting wildlife along the way. Applications are open 1–31 May each year, with 1,600 lucky winners drawn in June:
www.nps.gov/dena/planyourvisit/road-lottery.htm

WHILE YOU'RE THERE: Alaska has some of the best national parks in the country. Glacier Bay, part of Alaska's famed Inside Passage, with its stunning glaciers and marine life is the most popular and usually best seen from on-board a cruise ship or the local Marine Highway Ferry (*www.nps. gov/glba*). Or why not try the Gates of the Arctic, one of the least visited and hardest to reach national parks in the country, but also one of the most untouched and rewarding too: *www.nps.gov/gaar*

ARCHES NATIONAL PARK, UTAH

Imagine a land of red rock spires and soaring pinnacles the colour of flames, an alien world, closer in appearance to the surface of Mars than anywhere on Earth. Imagine thousands of stone arches, some spanning hundreds of feet across, changing colour with the shifting moods of the day: soft pink at sunrise, dulling to hard brown and then lighting up again, blazing hues of orange and amber as the setting sun casts shadows, like ghosts, across the high desert plains. This is Arches National Park; it's like being transported to another planet entirely.

Made up of 119 square miles of southern Utah's portion of the slick rock Colorado Plateau, the park contains over 2,000 natural sandstone arches, the largest concentration on Earth. There are cliff arches that cling to rock walls, pothole arches that look like natural skylights and freestanding ones that stretch across the landscape like stone rainbows. There are few places on the planet that have the sheer variety of geological features that Arches has: it's like looking at the world stripped bare, as if its skin – the grass and soil and greenery – has been ripped up and only the bones remain, twisted shapes, like sculptures, frozen in stone.

There are many rock stars here: the North Window, sun rising through it like a golden iris each morning; Delicate Arch, the largest in the park with an opening 46 feet tall and 32 feet wide, slick desert domes shining through from the other side; Landscape Arch, the longest on the planet, like a red ribbon stretched 306 feet across the mountainside; Balanced Rock, a gravity-defying 8.8-million-pound boulder, perched precariously on top of a thin tower, like the bending head of a petrified beast.

But although they may appear like sculptures, in reality, of course, they're not static at all. Arches is classed as a desert but it still receives on average eight to ten inches of precipitation a year. That rain soaks into the porous sandstone that makes up the arches here, dissolving the bonding between those ancient grains and splitting it from the inside out. In winter, water trapped in cracks turns to ice and slowly pries the rock apart like a vice. Wind plays a part too, gradually scouring away weak parts from the outside. Little by little, the incessant forces of nature mould the stone into ever changing forms that rise and fall, in imperceptible slow motion.

It has long been thought that the formations within the park were caused solely by this process of erosion, gradually undercutting the base of the rock or breaking off blocks from fractures within. But, it turns out, that's only part of the story. A team of scientists from the Czech Republic recently discovered that although certain material is washed away as predicted, the actual shapes of the arches, and other formations in the park, come not from the elements, but from inside the rock itself.

It has to do with stress. As individual grains of sand are

washed away, more pressure is placed on the ones that remain, causing them to interlock and become stronger. Think of it like a dry-stone wall. It's easy to take a brick off the top, but much harder to take one off the bottom because it's weighted – the bricks above push the lower ones down and keep them locked in place.

In the same way, erosion washes away the weak parts of the rock, but as it does so the weight shifts, causing certain areas to bear more pressure and therefore become stronger and harder to erode. Without that stress, that pressure from above, the entire landscape would have simply disappeared thousands of years ago. The weight binds the individual grains together into the solid forms we see today. But, in doing so, it also predetermines the shape the arch will eventually take. Blocks that begin with vertical cracks will one day produce columns and pinnacles; horizontal cracks produce arches and alcoves. Nature doesn't carve these forms from an infinite canvas, she's more like a palaeontologist dusting around a bone – the shape is designed by the rock itself, erosion just reveals what's already there.

That's what makes Arches special. It may feel like an alien landscape, but in fact it is quite the opposite. This is the Earth's sculpture garden; these are her designs. Here, in this desert of red stone, we find monuments carved by the forces of time, infinitely more amazing because they come not from the vision of a human eye, nor from the whims of wind and rain, but from the heart of the planet itself.

WHERE: Eastern central Utah, five miles north of Moab: *www.nps.gov/arch*

DON'T MISS: The sunrise though the North Window; get there early for the best view.

Photo: Luca Galuzzi

TOP TIP: Arches is a photographer's paradise. For the best light, check out Turret Arch, Double Arch and Landscape Arch in the early morning and Balanced Rock, Delicate Arch and the Devil's Garden in the late afternoon.

WHILE YOU'RE THERE: Stop by Canyonlands National Park, a vast expanse of dazzling red rock spires and snaking canyons just 30 minutes south of Arches. Take a picnic to the Green River Overlook and watch the sun set over the distant mesas – it'll be one of the most spectacular meals of your life: *www.nps.gov/cany*

DEATH VALLEY NATIONAL PARK, NEVADA

In 1849 a wagon train bound for California's gold fields took a deadly wrong turn. They had just left Salt Lake City, following the Old Spanish Trail around the southern end of the Sierra Nevada Mountains. The going was slow and tough. One day a young man rode into camp with a hand-sketched map that he claimed showed a shortcut that would cut 500 miles off their journey. There were 107 wagons in the train, many made up of families, women and children; most agreed to change course. It would be a decision that would cost many of them their lives.

Almost immediately they encountered difficulties. Over the next two months they crossed canyons and barren valleys, were saved from dehydration by a freak snowstorm, and eventually ended up, weak and lost, in what is now Travertine Hot Springs, in the centre of the park, trapped by the impenetrable wall of the Panamint Mountains before them and the desert they had just crossed behind. In desperation, they chose the two strongest men from their group to cross the mountains and get supplies. It would be almost a month before they returned. By then, only two families remained. As they left their camp and finally made their way west to safety, one of them is said to have looked back and proclaimed: 'Good-bye, Death Valley.'

The name stuck, but the moniker is unfair. This is indeed a place of extremes: the world record for the highest ever temperature, a baking 134 degrees Fahrenheit, was recorded here on 10 July 1913. In such heat, dying is easy – people fall over, sometimes just a short walk from their car, and never get up again; others drive into oblivion and never return.

But there is beauty here. Death Valley may conjure images of an ugly and desolate land, but the park is much more than just morbid desert. There are snow-capped peaks that rise to 11,000 feet and vast salt flats that sink to the lowest point on the continent, 282 feet below sea level. Sand dunes soar as tall as skyscrapers; hills are dyed like an artist's palette. There are golden badlands, slot canyons, even an enormous volcanic crater, 600 feet deep and half a mile across.

There's history too: old ghost towns like Rhyolite and Panamint City, once home to thousands, now abandoned to dust and sand; Barker Ranch where the infamous Manson family hid out during their killing spree. And mysteries as well: the Racetrack Playa, one of nature's great enigmas – enormous boulders that have somehow been dragged across the dried-out ground, seemingly by themselves or pushed by an invisible force.

Even in these extreme conditions, life exists here. Bighorn sheep wander the mountains for days without a drink; tortoises can go a year and bury themselves underground to stay cool; and the kangaroo rat, so perfectly adapted to this

desert environment, will not so much as wet its lips its entire life. There are lizards in the dunes; frogs in small pools; and tiny iridescent blue pupfish, the only known species of its kind in the world, that have survived for thousands of years, since the last Ice Age, only in Devil's Hole – a natural aquifer in a detached unit east of the park that goes down at least 435 feet (as far as divers have explored to date) and probably much deeper.

The park's microbial life is even more interesting. Exobiologists, the scientists charged with discovering extraterrestrial life, study the microscopic organisms that thrive in some of Death Valley's most inhospitable locations, flourishing without light and oxygen in ground that can reach 200 degrees Fahrenheit. If you can make it here, the theory goes, you can make it anywhere – even, perhaps, on Mars, whose landscape billions of years ago would have resembled something close to Death Valley today.

But the most striking example of life's tenacity are the wildflowers. Modest blooms happen every year, but once every decade or so the valley receives a deluge of brief, extreme rain that causes a 'superbloom', turning the parched pale land into a rainbow of shimmering colour: sunflowers of desert gold and petals of bright lavender carpet the valley floor; white gravel ghosts and clusters of scarlet paintbrushes crowd the hillsides.

In her 1922 book about the valley, *The White Heart of Mojave*, the adventurer Edna Brush Perkins wrote: 'The desert mixes up your ideas about what you call living and dying. You see the dreadful, dead country living in beauty, and feel that the silence pressing around it is alive.' Even here, in the midst of death's grip, there is magnificence and colour; even here, life is defiant still.

WHERE: Inyo County, California, 120 miles west of Las Vegas and 260 miles north of Los Angeles. There are numerous gateway towns depending on where you enter. See website for details: *www.nps.gov/deva*

DON'T MISS: Zabriskie Point at sunrise, or sunset, for stunning views of the multi-coloured hills of the badlands.

TOP TIP: For the best chance of witnessing a superbloom year of wildflowers, watch the weather: a big autumn rainstorm is a good indicator, but they'll need to be regularly above average rainfall throughout the winter too. Come late March to early April when the park starts to warm up and check the national park website's wildflower page for predictions.

WHILE YOU'RE THERE: Stop by Joshua Tree National Park, 250 miles to the south, where the Mojave and the Colorado deserts meet in a surreal display of spectacular trees and dramatic wind-sculpted rocks: *www.nps.gov/jotr*

EVERGLADES NATIONAL PARK, FLORIDA

The writer Greg Guirard said: 'There's something about being out in the swamp ... that seems to suck the poisons of civilisation out of you, some sort of healing power that allows you to begin to be yourself again.' He was referring to the bayous of Louisiana, but he might as well as have been talking about the Everglades. There is vitality here, a freshness that clears the cobwebs from city-stricken souls.

Biodiversity is the key. The writer Marjory Stoneman Douglas called the Everglades a 'River of Grass'; and so it is, a vast moving swathe of marshy hideaways flowing 100 miles through the southern central part of the state. In total, there are nine distinct habitats within the park's 2,410 square miles, including the largest sub-tropical wilderness reserve on the continent, the largest stand of sawgrass prairie in the country and the largest protected mangrove forest in the Northern Hemisphere; as well as deep estuaries, dense stands of hardwood hammocks, pine rocklands and more. These interconnected ecosystems support a staggering variety of life – more than 360 species of birds, 40 types of mammals and 50 classes of reptile call the Everglades home, including the highest concentration of wading birds in America – enough to 'block out light from the sun' as one 19th-century naturalist, John James Audubon, put it.

But what's even more unusual is its location. The park sits on the border of temperate American and subtropical Caribbean ecosystems, meaning flora and fauna that don't normally co-exist together can be found here side by side. Hawks, bobcats and the elusive Florida panther – one of the most endangered animals on Earth – rub shoulders with loggerhead turtles, flamingos and the smiling, puppy dog face of the West Indian Manatee. But the most vivid example of the park's unique blend of wildlife are the alligators and crocodiles – gators from the North share water with crocs from the South, the only place in the world where you can see both in a single glance. And it's one you won't forget: direct descendents of the dinosaurs, with teeth like daggers and a merciless green stare, to look one in the eye is to confront a real-life monster face to face; to feel, for the briefest of moments, truly vulnerable, rolled in its jaws and dragged to the river bed.

There's history too. Before the Spanish arrived in 1513, this region was home to one of the most remarkable Native American tribes in the country. The Calusa Indians were an aggressive people, tall and muscular, with long black hair, feared by neighbouring tribes and the invading Spanish alike. But they were also smart, controlling this enormous stretch of the Florida peninsula for more than 2,000 years. They built a vast network of as many as 50 Gulf Coast villages, digging out canals by hand and terraforming their environment in order to thrive. At their peak, their population reached as many as 50,000 – an enormous, complex society that collected shells for tools and architectural material, fished for mullet, catfish and turtle, and travelled by hollowed-out cypress log canoes up and down their waterways, much as we do today.

But, perhaps, the most important story of the park is its conservation. Established in 1947, the Everglades was the first national park of its time that was set up solely to protect the diversity of its plant and animal life, rather than its scenic beauty. It was a ground-breaking moment in conservation – a wilderness area set aside for its own sake, rather than its benefits to human kind. But that foresight is also tragically ironic. Today the Everglades are one of the most threatened ecosystems in the country. Upstream urban development and agricultural run-off from chemical fertilisers are poisoning the watery habitats of the park; man-made canals restrict its natural flow; and the human pressures are mounting – the creatures of the Everglades must coexist with over 6 million human beings on their borders; and we do not share well.

But there is hope. One of the largest conservation projects in history is already underway. Made up of over 50 individual projects, the Comprehensive Everglades Restoration Plan (CERP), which was initially drafted to cost more than $10

Photo: Marc Ryckaert (MJJR)

billion, has been designed to re-establish the correct balance of water flow through the wider Everglades ecosystem, addressing the primary cause of ecosystem degradation. Historically over 450 billion gallons of water flowed through Everglades National Park annually; today that number is less than 260 billion. Completion isn't expected until sometime in the 2030s, and as always money and resources are tight – the fight is still on, but if it can prove successful it would be a marker for future ecosystem restoration programmes around the world. The Everglades will be sucking the poisons of civilisation out of its waters again soon.

WHERE: Southern Florida. The nearest towns are Homestead, for the main entrance to the east of the park; Flamingo, in the south-west; and Everglades City in the north: *www.nps.gov/ever*

DON'T MISS: Air boats are a fun and popular way to see the park, with the benefit of covering a lot of territory in a short space of time. But for a quieter, more intimate Everglades experience consider following part of the 100-mile Wilderness Waterway, a long-distance canoe/kayak trail that bisects the park from north to south. Make the most of prevailing winds in winter and early spring by starting in Everglades City and finishing in Flamingo, camping out over the water each night on elevated wooden platforms, called 'chickees'. Expect to paddle roughly ten miles per day. Good navigation and backcountry experience required.

TOP TIP: Interested in cold war history? Join a ranger-led tour of the park's secret attraction: an abandoned anti-aircraft missile site that was built in response to the 1962 Cuban missile crisis. Only available December–April.

WHILE YOU'RE THERE: Visit the Dry Tortugas National Park, 70 miles off the coast of Key West, just a short day cruise away. Composed of seven small islands the park contains a spectacular civil war era fort, a vast assortment of bird life and some of the best snorkelling and scuba diving in the country: *www.nps.gov/drto*

HAWAI'I VOLCANOES NATIONAL PARK, BIG ISLAND, HAWAI'I

Volcanoes are world builders. As magma from deep beneath the Earth's mantle is pumped up to the surface it cools on impact with the air or sea, solidifying and gradually forming new landmasses. By current count, over 80 per cent of the Earth's surface was formed by volcanic activity; and gas from ancient eruptions may also have been instrumental in helping to stitch together the first molecular building blocks of life. They are more than fire and brimstone, more than raw power. Volcanoes are the fountain of existence; a reminder that our planet is ever changing and we, mere blushes on its skin.

Which is why Hawai'i Volcanoes National Park is so remarkable. Located on the Big Island of Hawai'i, these 505 square miles of lush rainforest and cooled jet-black lava flows are one of the best places in the world to see volcanic activity up close. Indeed, the Hawaiian islands themselves were formed by ongoing volcanic eruptions at the seabed, gradually piling layer upon layer of cooled lava on top of itself until the stack broke the surface of the ocean and created the archipelago we see today. And it's not finished

Photo: Bob Linsdell

yet. In the last 35 years, volcanic activity has added roughly 500 acres of new land to the Big Island and there's more to come. Being here is, quite literally, like watching the birth of a new world.

Kīlauea is the park's biggest star. One of the world's most active volcanoes, erupting near continuously for over 30 years, in its centre is an enormous lava lake bordered by an eight-mile-wide caldera with 400-foot walls on all sides. Legend has it, this is the home of Pele, the Hawaiian goddess of volcanoes. In local dialect her name is 'Ka wahine `ai honua', the woman who devours the land. Eruptions are seen as an expression of her fiery temper and the passion for her long-lost love. She is the creator here, but also the destroyer. In 1983, a four-mile long fissure opened on her east rift zone shooting a fountain of lava 1,500 feet into the air – roughly the height of the Empire State Building. Peer inside today and it's like looking into a giant witch's cauldron; a fiery brew of bubbling red hot lava and churning molten rock, charged from the depths of the Earth itself.

Kīlauea may steal the show, but her sister dwarfs her in size. Measuring 60 miles long and twenty miles wide, the enormous Mauna Loa volcano takes up more than half of the island, rising 13,680 feet above sea level and then continuing under water for over double that height, before compressing the sea bed with its colossal weight for a further five miles. The total height of Mauna Loa, from the ocean floor to its summit, is roughly 56,000 feet – almost twice the height of Mount Everest – making it the largest mountain mass on the planet, some 19,000 cubic miles in total, big enough to hold at least 3,000 Mount St Helens in its massive frame. And it's still active. Over the last 3,000 years Mauna Loa has erupted on average every six years. Her last was in 1984 when molten lava seeped through cracks in her side and exploded into the air, leaking iridescent rivers of fire into the sea. She's been taking a nap, but not for long.

But it's not just about the volcanoes. Located 2,000 miles from the nearest continental land mass, the Hawaiian archipelago is the most geographically isolated place on Earth. The plants and animals that live here have evolved in complete separation from the rest of the world, arriving by water, wind or wing millions of years ago. Today, these islands have the highest level of endemism that can be found anywhere on the planet – even the Galápagos. Some 90 per cent of the terrestrial flora and fauna in the park – songbirds, turtles, dragonflies and more – can be found here and nowhere else on Earth.

There is cultural history too. On the southern flank of Kīlauea, about sixteen miles from its rim, is Puʻu Loa, a sacred site for the indigenous people of Hawaiʻi where over 23,000 petroglyphs have been carved into the dark lava stone: geometric shapes of circles and dimples, human figures and sailing canoes. Nearby, are a set of 200-year-old footprints preserved in the hardened ash of the Kaʻū Desert, thought to be from a band of warriors travelling on a raid to a nearby village – their last.

Adventure is everywhere – from hikes along the Crater Rim Trail passing through rainforests and desert landscapes of black volcanic basalt, to treks to distant lookouts where red-hot magma steams slowly into the sea. There are giant hollowed lava tubes to explore, scenic drives and backcountry camping on the summit of the biggest volcano in the world. But in the end, it's those quiet moments of reflection that matter most: the fire and brimstone, the raw power, creators and destroyers, goddesses, building worlds beneath our feet.

WHERE: Big Island, Hawaiʻi. The nearest town is Volcano

Village, just five minutes from the main entrance: *www.nps.gov/havo*

DON'T MISS: Kīlauea's fiery crater at night – one of the most spectacular ways to see the awesome colours of the volcano in action. Almost zero light pollution makes for a stunning starscape too. Book a room in Volcano House, the only accommodation in the park, for easy access and rooms boasting crater views: *www.hawaiivolcanohouse.com*

TOP TIP: Beware of the curse: it is said that if you steal volcanic rocks from the park, the goddess Pele, who lives in the crater of the Kīlauea volcano, will inflict bad luck upon you. Whether you believe the legend or not, hundreds of pieces of lava rock are mailed back to the island each year from travellers who claim to have suffered misfortune since they tried to steal a souvenir home. Also, be sure to check out the Hawaiian Volcano Observatory website for regular updates on Kīlauea and Mauna Loa's eruption status: *http://hvo.wr.usgs.gov*

WHILE YOU'RE THERE: It's not exactly close (nothing is), but why not combine a trip to Hawai'i Volcanoes National Park with a trip to Crater Lake National Park, in Oregon. It's considered by many to be one of the most beautiful lakes in the country and, because it's formed from a volcanic caldera, ties in perfectly with the geology of Kīlauea and Mauna Loa too. Direct flights from Portland to Honolulu make it an easy stopover for most people travelling from the States: *www.nps.gov/crla*

MAMMOTH CAVE NATIONAL PARK, KENTUCKY

Mammoth Cave National Park, deep in the hill country of southern central Kentucky, is home to the longest known cave system in the world. Legend has it, that it was discovered in 1797 when a frontiersman, named John Houchin, came upon a black bear and shot it. But he missed (proving, some locals say, he couldn't have been a real Kentuckian). The bear chased him through the forest and eventually led him to the entrance of what is now Mammoth Cave, where he escaped into the darkness inside.

Since that day, more than 200 years ago, the cave has been explored extensively, by adventurers, tourists, scientists and more, but the end still hasn't been reached. Roughly 400 miles of underground labyrinth has been revealed to date, but the total length could reach 1,000 miles or more – dwarfing, by far, the length of any other known cave system in the world. But it won't be easy to get there. Even with sophisticated modern technology, experts predict it could take another 100 years to survey the cave in its entirety, such is the arduousness and complexity of the task. Mammoth's secrets are hidden in the dark and she's not sharing them easily.

The problem is getting there. Imagine sliding on your belly 1,000 feet through a crevice so narrow that your back scrapes the ceiling with every inch. Imagine darkness so complete that it envelops all your senses, a living, menacing thing that peers over your shoulder and whispers dangers in your ear. To reach the far unexplored corners of Mammoth Cave requires climbing, crawling, wading through cold dripping depths and dirt; it means getting lost, with little chance of rescue, lowering yourself into pitch blackness, 30 hours

Photo: Dave Bunnell

underground without rest. This is the abyss, a world of cold danger and primal fear abandoned by light and life above.

But it's also beautiful. The features inside the cave, many of them named, are like sculptures on a gallery wall. The flowstone of Frozen Niagara, like sheets of rain petrified in mid-fall; the Rotunda, one of the largest caverns in the system, tapestries of rock swirling like frescos above. There are passages lined with gypsum flowers, subterranean canyons adorned with dripstone and statue-like stalactites and stalagmites that have been carved continuously, drop by drop, every second of every day, for hundreds of thousands of years. Fossils line the walls. The rock here was once the bed of a shallow saltwater sea – there are gastropods, crinoids, even the teeth of ancient sharks embedded in stone. One of the cave's earliest guides, a slave by the name of Stephen Bishop, described it as a 'grand, gloomy and peculiar place' – and so it is: Mammoth is raw, not dressed up, but somehow more beautiful for that. A vast masterpiece of nature carved in the endless creativity of time.

The history is just as interesting too. Thousands of years before that bear Native Americans travelled miles into the cave, using cane plants as torches, in order to collect minerals for medicinal and ceremonial uses. Hundreds of artefacts, perfectly preserved in the controlled temperature and humidity of the cave, have been discovered: gourd bowls, pottery and petroglyphs.

Centuries later, those early frontiersmen, like Houchins, quickly learned that the cave possessed enormous quantities of saltpetre, which was used in the making of gunpowder. A commercial factory was established here during the war of 1812. Vats and wooden pipes, left behind from the operation, can still be seen to this day. Later still, in 1842, an ill-fated hospital was opened in the cave with the thought that its unique environmental conditions would cure tuberculosis. It didn't, of course, and lasted less than a year – most of its patients, and its founder, dying from the disease before they could realise the error of their idea.

By 1838 tourists began arriving. Stephen Bishop, and other slaves, were tasked with leading the tours – some as long as fourteen hours. Bishop, particularly, would achieve nationwide fame for his knowledge and bravery, crossing a terrifying section of the cave known as the Bottomless Pit for the first time and opening up large parts for further exploration.

Today, a number of tours are available, all guided, from easy 30-minute jaunts to day-long expeditions that require technical climbing, long strenuous hikes and a head (and belly) for small spaces (one section requires squeezing through a ninc-inch-tall passage). Whichever you choose, if you're brave, and lucky, at one point your guide will turn off the lights, allowing you to experience, for just an instant, the absolute, all-consuming presence of true darkness. Then, suddenly, a match is struck and the magic of light is revealed. From that one small flame, shadows retreat and the colours of the Earth's longest cave are revealed: tapestries of time, secrets yet to be revealed. The world above ground will never feel the same again.

WHERE: Edmonson County, Kentucky, 89 miles south of Louisville. The nearest town is Park City: *www.nps.gov/maca*

DON'T MISS: The Violet City Lantern Tour, where historic oil-lamps are used for lighting, instead of electric lamps, in order to recreate the atmosphere and colours experienced by the early explorers.

TOP TIPS: Watch out for ghosts. Mammoth Cave has over 150 documented paranormal events, many of them experienced by credible witnesses, including rangers and scientists.

WHILE YOU'RE THERE: Stop by the Great Smoky Mountains National Park, less than an hour south of Knoxville, Tennessee, and only four hours east of Mammoth Cave: rolling mountains covered in blue tints of early morning mist and some of the best autumnal colours in the country: *www.nps.gov/grsm*

BANFF NATIONAL PARK, ALBERTA

Canada's first national park was discovered by accident. In 1883, three rail workers stumbled across a cave filled with natural hot springs while surveying routes for the Canada Pacific Railway's coast-to-coast line – one of the most ambitious engineering projects of the time. They described the scene as a: 'fantastic dream from a tale of the Arabian Nights'. Mist poured down the mountain slopes; steam and bubbling hot water billowed from within. By 1885 the Canadian government had claimed it as a nature reserve, but its boundaries soon expanded to encompass more than 2,564 square miles and become Canada's first national park. It was one of the most important discoveries of the time, setting off a chain reaction that has now led to the creation of over 40 national parks and reserves in the country, from the far reaches of the Canadian arctic to the fjords of the wild east coast. But those three rail workers could never have imagined the true majesty of what they found.

Banff has it all: fairy-tale mountains, emerald lakes and glaciers that stretch like icy fingers across the jagged land. If you want to experience the true awe of the mountains, the magnitude of Mother Earth and the unfathomable vastness and beauty of her hand, Banff National Park is the place to go. Even better, for many, is its accessibility. While many national parks require some sweat to see them at their best (though that will benefit you here too), Banff requires nothing but open eyes and a beating heart. The most breathtaking mountain scenery in the world, just a few steps from your car – and it changes on every bend.

Start with the water. Locals joke that they have to repaint the lakebeds each year, such is the brilliance of their colour, but they might as well be telling the truth. In summer, light refracts off glacial minerals in the water creating pools of almost impossibly bright turquoise. Lake Louise is the most famous – a gigantic emerald embedded in the Earth, with snow-capped summits rising to 11,000 feet all around. In summer, paddle out in dawn silence or hike trails around its rim; in winter, skate on its frozen surface. But there are others too: Moraine Lake, equally as vivid, set in the Valley of the Ten Peaks with a ring of rugged summits above, like sharpened mountain teeth; and Lake Minnewanka, the largest at thirteen miles long, feared and respected by the indigenous Stoney Nakoda First Nations people as a place where spirits dwell. They may be right: come on a clear winter's night and it's one of the best places in the park to witness the lights of the Aurora dancing across the sky above.

Deeper in the park there are canyons filled with lush forests and raging waterfalls; rivers that bubble with rapids and others that meander with lazy flows. Some of the best ski terrain in North America is here, steep fast lines that fall into mesmerizing views. There are opportunities for

Photo: Gorgo

dog sledding, snow-shoeing, trekking, biking, camping and walking on glaciers – even scuba diving among the remains of a submerged lake village. Those same hot springs, discovered in 1883, are still open year round too, piped up from almost two miles into the Earth's crust at a sweltering 116 degrees Fahrenheit.

Then there's the Icefields Parkway, 143 miles of ever-changing grandeur connecting Banff with its neighbouring national park, Jasper – colossal vistas filled with vivid colour on every corner, like driving through a film set with a shifting backdrop. Elk, deer and bighorn sheep line the slopes; there are bears, moose and wolves hiding within.

The former Prime Minister of Canada, Sir John A. Macdonald, said in 1887: 'I do not suppose, in any part of the world there can be found a spot, taken all together, which combines so many attractions.' He's still right to this day. The greatness of Banff National Park is not just in its jaw-dropping scenery, but in its variety. Here is a place where all nature's elements come together as one, where every conceivable adventure is on hand and wonder is as easy to find as opening your eyes and listening to your heart.

WHERE: Alberta, Canada, 87 miles west of Calgary. The gateway town is Banff itself: *www.pc.gc.ca/en/pn-np/ab/banff*

DON'T MISS: If you can afford it, book a night at the Fairmont Chateau Lake Louise, an elegant mountain resort, built over 100 years ago on the shores of the lake, with the best views in the park: *www.fairmont.com/lake-louise*

TOP TIP: The lakes change colour throughout the year – come in July and August to see them at their most dazzling. This time of year also offers the best weather, but the biggest crowds. If you're after solitude, but still want to do summer activities, mid-September through to early October is your best bet.

WHILE YOU'RE THERE: Connected to Banff are a number of other national parks and reserves, just a short drive away. Jasper (*www.pc.gc.ca/en/pn-np/ab/jasper*), the largest in the country, at 4,200 square miles, with scenery just as big; and Yoho (*www.pc.gc.ca/en/pn-np/bc/yoho*) – a Cree Indian exclamation of awe – less crowded with alpine meadows, sharp angular peaks and one of the most significant fossils troves on Earth, are two of the best.

GWAII HAANAS NATIONAL PARK RESERVE, BRITISH COLUMBIA

The Haida Gwaii archipelago, a string of more than 150 mist-covered islands 62 miles off the northern coast of British Columbia, is unlike anywhere else on Earth. Home of the Haida people for at least the last 12,500 years, regular dousings of thick rain have blessed the land with abundance. Lush forests of cedar and Sitka spruce, dripping in moss, tower like skyscrapers hundreds of feet above the ground; bald eagles soar through the sky; the bays swell with salmon, sea lions and orca whales. Life is richer here, more wild and vast. This isn't a destination; it's a feeling: a land of giants and myths, a glimpse at how alive the world really is, and a promise of what it can one day still be.

The national park, whose name Gwaii Haanas means 'islands of wonder' in native tongue, comprises roughly 15 per cent of the region, 138 islands in total. Coming here is a retreat from the modern world. There is no mobile phone signal, no stores or roads. Time slows to the pace of the tides, the rhythm of the forest. There is an immediate serenity, a sense of balance and life lived in harmony with the land, that comes from the Haida people themselves. They are the soul of the park and its guardians. But they had to fight for its existence.

In 1985, frustrated by the relentless logging of their homeland and the seemingly hopeless bureaucratic process to protect it, the Haida people banded together, linking arms to form a blockade against logging equipment and roads. Seventy two were arrested in total, many of them elders dressed in ceremonial regalia, saying they had no choice but to protect the land for their unborn grandchildren. The protest gained national attention and only lasted two weeks before the country had seen enough. Two years later, in 1987, the Gwaii Haanas National Park Reserve and Haida Heritage Site was officially created – a direct result of the blockade – with the vision that it would be co-managed by the park service and the Haida people themselves – an award-winning model that has proved an inspiration for other aboriginal people around the world. More recently, a National Marine Conservation Area Reserve has been added to extend the park six miles off shore – the only place on the planet where an entire landscape, from mountain summit to ocean bed, is protected.

It's a good job too, for these islands of wonder are one of the most ecologically rich places on Earth, known locally as the 'Galápagos of the North'. Isolation from the mainland and its unique position on the edge of the continental shelf has created an extremely high level of endemism: at least 39 species of plant and animal exist here and nowhere else on the planet, including the unique Haida Gwaii black bear, the largest black bear in North America, with jaws adapted to feasting on the hard shelled sea creatures that live by the water's edge.

But perhaps most impressive is the sheer abundance of life itself. Half of the 1.5 million seabirds that nest in the archipelago make their home in the national park; millions more pass through on seasonal migrations each year. There are bright tufted puffins bobbing for fish in the open water, great blue herons standing like statues in the shallows and more eagle nests per mile of shoreline than anywhere else in the country. Nutrient-rich waters attract sea lions, dolphins, porpoises and whales in astounding numbers. Take a kayak out on the water (it is one of the best places in the world for doing so) and it would not be uncommon to share the ocean with dozens of migrating humpback whales, arching their backs, breaching the surface as their blow holes exhale the sea. For fisherman it is a paradise too: bays overflow with salmon, halibut, crab and shrimp. In one place, Burnaby Narrows, a 150-foot-wide ocean channel, there is thought to be more biomass per volume, more life itself, than in any other intertidal zone on Earth. Deer ghost through forests; bears forage on the deserted sandy shores. Being here is, quite simply, one of the greatest wildlife experiences on Earth.

But in the end, it is, perhaps, the Haida people themselves that leave the most lasting impression. Master artists and carvers, a once fierce people that now passionately defend their land and way of life. The park today protects more than 500 Haida heritage sites, including the ancient village of Nang Sdins Llnagaay, on the island of SGang Gwaay, where a spectacular collection of carved monumental poles still stand, slowly returning to the soil, as is the Haida tradition,

Photo: Susan Womersley

consumed by the relentless sea-wind and rain. To be here is to feel their deep connection to the land first hand, the land they fought for and won, a place of giants, a retreat from the modern world, where time ebbs with the rhythms of the forest and tides of the sea.

WHERE: The north-west coast of British Columbia, Canada, 434 miles north of Vancouver. The nearest town is Sandspit: *www.pc.gc.ca/en/pn-np/bc/gwaiihaanas*

DON'T MISS: Kayaking with orcas, grey whales and humpbacks, one of the world's great marine adventures. The season for spotting them runs May to October, with July and August usually offering the best chances and the driest weather.

TOP TIP: The best way to see the archipelago is from the water. To get the most out of your trip consider a small ship liveaboard cruise or multi-day kayaking adventure, camping out on deserted beaches along the way. Moresby Explorers and Maple Leaf Adventures are two of the best operators.

WHILE YOU'RE THERE: Combine a trip to the Haida Gwaii with a visit to the Great Bear Rainforest, just a few hours from Vancouver – the only place in the world to see the mysterious all-white Kermode, or Spirit Bear – and also one of the best places to witness grizzlies feasting on the annual salmon run. Come late August to middle of October for the best chance of spotting both: *https://greatbearrainforest.gov.bc.ca*

WAPUSK NATIONAL PARK, MANITOBA

The far north of Canada is a stark and beautiful land. To stand on the edge of the ice-flow, to feel the arctic winds, the great freeze fading to the endless horizon, is to look the abyss in the eye and know, beyond a doubt, that these lands are outside the grasp of human civilisation and control. There is a wildness here, a danger, unlike anywhere else on Earth.

But Wapusk, which means 'white bear' in native Cree, is special for other reasons too. Located 25 miles south-east of Churchill, on the shores of the Hudson Bay, these 4,431 square miles of ice and high alpine tundra are home to one of the world's largest known polar bear denning sites. It is here that these great white bears come to birth and raise their young.

Supporting a population of roughly 1,000, the bears follow a seasonal pattern – mating in summer, migrating along the coast in autumn in search of pack ice and seals, feasting all winter, then returning to land with the spring melt. Pregnant females are different. Rather than spending the winter on the sea ice hunting, they build dens here in the surrounding area of the national park, hollowing out caves in snowdrifts where they will raise their young. From late October until mid-February the mother bear will nurse her cubs, hidden inside the den. When they finally emerge the true magic of Wapusk is on display – dozens of three-month-old polar bears taking their first steps in the snow, learning the skills they will need to survive in one of the world's most inhospitable environments.

They are remarkable animals. Adult male polar bears can reach 1,300 pounds, sprint at over 30 miles per hour,

Photo: Ansgar Walk

Photo: Ansgar Walk

swim for up to 60 miles at a time and sniff out a seal twenty miles away. They're smart too, with a comparable level of intelligence to a great ape. Inuit folklore recounts tales of polar bears covering their dark noses with a paw to remain camouflaged while hunting, they have been seen using blocks of ice as tools to smash into seal nurseries and they are highly skilled hunters, waiting motionless by breathing holes for up to fourteen hours at a time.

But there's other magic here too. The park is home to the arctic fox, wolves and over 200 species of bird, including great grey owls and flocks of snow geese flying overhead. In spring, the north-east of the park turns into an enormous nursery for caribou, part of one of the largest animal migrations on the planet when herds, hundreds of thousands strong, travel between their winter feeding and spring calving grounds. In summer, visitors can also don dry suits and swim with beluga whales in nearby Churchill. Nicknamed 'sea canaries' for their distinctive high-pitched whistles and ability to mimic the sounds around them – including human speech, they are one of the smartest, most friendly marine animals on the planet and the Hudson Bay coastline is home to the world's largest population – roughly 57,000 gather here between mid-June and mid-September each year.

It is not always just ice: in summer, berries and wildflowers fill the ground with colour and the midnight sun casts a pale glow over the land. There are taiga forests, rushing rivers, salt marshes, ancient beaches and, above it all, the dancing colours of the Aurora Borealis. With displays of the Northern Lights 300 days a year, Wapusk is one of the top three places on the planet to witness this awe-inspiring wonder of the natural world.

There's history as well. The Inuit, Cree and Dene have used this region as a seasonal hunting ground for over 3,000 years. Come today and you can still experience much of their culture first hand – from traditional dog sledding expeditions across the frozen tundra to listening to aboriginal stories around the campfire at night.

But perhaps most important is what the park is showing us. Sea ice extent has declined 13 per cent per decade since records began. Polar bear populations, which depend on the sea ice for survival, are down 22 per cent. It is here that climate change packs its first, and arguably hardest, punch: pollution. And increased industrialisation from oil and gas exploration packs the second. The polar bears are, literally, losing the ground beneath their feet. If we're not careful, we'll lose something else too: the stark and desolate beauty of the far North, that danger, that wild allure, and the chance to see the great white kings who still rule this icy land.

WHERE: Manitoba, Canada, on the western shore of the Hudson Bay, 25 miles south-east of Churchill, the gateway to the park: *www.pc.gc.ca/en/pn-np/mb/wapusk*

DON'T MISS: Seeing the annual polar bear congregation along the coast late October to early November and the cubs emerging from their dens mid-February to mid-March.

TOP TIP: Wat'chee Lodge, located just outside the park boundaries, only opens four weeks a year when the mother bears and cubs are emerging from their dens. A secret of professional wildlife photographers and nature lovers, it is right in the heart of the denning area and the best base from which to watch the magic unfold: *http://watchee.com*

WHILE YOU'RE THERE: There are no roads to Churchill, the nearest town to Wapusk National Park, so most people fly from Winnipeg. Extend your stay with a visit to Riding Mountain National Park, just three hours west of the city. A patchwork of prairie land, boreal forest and lake beaches filled with black bear, bison and bugling elk: perfect for a couple of days hiking, fishing and wildlife spotting: *www.pc.gc.ca/en/pn-np/mb/riding*

SOUTH AMERICA

THE GALÁPAGOS NATIONAL PARK, ECUADOR

Nowhere else does a place so tiny pack such a big punch. The Galapágos Islands are less than half the size of Hawaiʻi, but they have changed the way we think about life on this planet more profoundly than anywhere else in the world.

The reason is isolation. Located 600 miles off the coast of Ecuador, in the middle of the Pacific Ocean, the creatures that make their home here have been completely cut off from the rest of the world for millions of years. As a result, these twenty small islands have one of the highest levels of endemism anywhere on the planet. It's like a little world in itself. Galápagos giant tortoises, marine iguanas, the Galápagos penguin and many more utterly unique species can be seen here and nowhere else on the planet. In total, a staggering 97 per cent of the reptiles and land mammals, 80 per cent of the land birds, 30 per cent of the plants and 20 per cent of the marine life are completely unique to this tiny island chain.

That fact caught the eye of a certain 19th-century naturalist.

The HMS Beagle arrived in the Galápagos Islands on 15 September, 1835, as part of a five-year exploratory journey around the globe. At the time, Charles Darwin was a relative novice. They stayed six weeks and he spent nineteen days ashore collecting specimens and making observations in his journal. But despite his youth (he was 22 years old when they set sail) and inexperience he noticed something no one had seen before. Although the ecosystem for the Galápagos as a whole was near identical, there were stark differences between individual species of the same genus from island to island. The finch that existed on one island was not the same as the finch that existed on another. The shells of one island's tortoise were completely distinct from the shells from another island. If all species are immutable, created whole by a divine act (as was the prevailing view at the time) how could these slight variations in the same species be possible?

His answer, in the book *On the Origin of Species*, published after his return to England in 1859, was simple and profound. In it, he proved the high level of endemism of each island – that there were unique sub-sets of species pertaining to each place that were specific to that island alone. But at the same time, he also showed how each of these unique species was closely related. Rather than assume that each one of these variations was a completely new type of animal, he argued that they were in fact the same species, which had diverged over time due to the minute behavioural and climatic conditions across the different islands. Living beings, Darwin argued, are not static things, created whole by God; they adapt to their environment; they change. We don't just exist, we evolve.

It was an utterly radical idea, but it stuck, explaining all the innumerable observations of life on this planet with unprecedented elegance and simplicity and setting a path

for natural science that we are still following to this day. To stand on the shores where Darwin collected his samples, to ponder the mysteries these islands have unlocked is powerful. But for most visitors it's just the start.

The true magic of the Galápagos is not in the type of animals that live here, but in their behaviour. It has to do with isolation again. The first person to set foot on the islands was the Dominican friar, Fray Tomás de Berlanga, the Bishop of Panama, in 1535, after his ship was set off course by strong currents. In the 17th century pirates used the Galápagos as a hideout and source of fresh water and food. Other than that, for all the eons of history that the islands have existed, apart from a few shipwrecks, botanists and, since the 1930s, a steadily growing number of tourists, there has been extremely limited human contact.

As a result, the wildlife here does not view human beings as a threat; they're a curiosity. Come and you will swim with sea lions, play with penguins and walk through enormous bird colonies without so much as ruffling a feather. Mockingbirds will perch on your shoulder; waved albatrosses (another endemic species, who famously kiss each other's beaks while mating) will waddle up and say hi. There is no other animal experience on the planet that allows such intimacy. This isn't just another safari, another glimpse at creatures running scared at first sight of Earth's alpha predator. This is the world without man, the planet untainted by human touch.

Wildlife is undoubtedly the star, but there are other highlights too. The island of Santa Cruz is the central cog for most itineraries, home of mangrove swamps teeming with black-tip sharks and misty forests where giant Galápagos tortoises roam free. On Isabella, the biggest island of the chain, you can trek up the Sierra Negra volcano – the second largest caldera in the world – one day and kayak around Tagus

Cove, where the names of pirates are still carved in the rock, the next. There are islands where you can hike through lava tunnels, beaches with world-class surf breaks (note: the sea lions may surf with you) and, almost everywhere, the chance to snorkel and dive some of the clearest, most abundant waters on Earth – the Galápagos Islands are as adventurous as you want to make it.

But the greatest adventure is what happens inside. To glimpse the world unaffected by human hands, to be accepted as an equal by the ecosystem, not feared as a predator, is a life-changing experience. And it's only possible here, on these tiny specks of rocks, lost for millions of years in the middle of the Pacific; a world within a world; a place unlike anywhere else on Earth. Come, and like Darwin, you'll return convinced that the world is more amazing than you had ever previously imagined.

WHERE: Six hundred miles off the west coast of Ecuador; the island of Santa Cruz is the main tourist hub. Flights daily from Quito via Guayaquil: *www.galapagos.org*
www.ecuador.travel/destination/galapagos-islands-ecuador

DON'T MISS: The Charles Darwin Research Station, on the island of Santa Cruz, home of the Galápagos Islands' scientific and conservation efforts – including a captive breeding programme for giant tortoises, one of the region's most iconic species:*www.darwinfoundation.org/en*

TOP TIP: Most people see the Galápagos on an organised cruise, but for a more cost effective option consider a land-based stay. The range of islands that can be explored is usually less, but with careful planning and regular day trips out to sea, it's still possible to experience many of the region's main highlights. Puerto Villamil, on the island of Isabela, is a wonderfully laid-back beach town and excellent base for trips further afield.

WHILE YOU'RE THERE: Most international flights to the Galápagos connect in Quito, Ecuador. Make sure to spend a few days here exploring the Inca history of the city, the cloud forest on its doorstep and the spectacular Cotopaxi National Park, just 31 miles to the south-east, home of wild horses, spectacled bears (perfect for *Paddington Bear* fans) and one of the most breathtakingly beautiful volcanoes in the world: *www.ecuador.travel/destination/andes/quito*

TORRES DEL PAINE NATIONAL PARK, CHILE

At the southern tip of South America is a land of mountain spires and pale blue ice; a boundless land, carved by glaciers, desolate and wild, but virtually untouched and unrivalled in grandeur and scale by almost anywhere else on the planet. Covering 400,000 square miles of Argentina and Chile, bigger than the entire United Kingdom combined, this vast expanse of emerald forests and sapphire lakes, where westerly winds blow strong enough to knock a man from his feet, is the last frontier of the American continent. Bruce Chatwin, the legendary travel writer who made his name here, described it as: 'the farthest place to which man walked from his place of origin'. Whispered by travellers and explorers in hushed, mythical tones, a place where your wildest dreams of adventure are dwarfed by the staggering colour around you; this land has a name, it's called Patagonia.

There are many highlights. On the Argentinian side, the north-east coast is filled with pods of orcas, southern right whales, elephant seals and the world's largest colony of Magellanic penguins: 210,000 breeding pairs take residence on the beaches around Punta Tombo from September to March each year. Further south, the spectacular Los Glaciares National Park, highlighted in the next chapter of this book, emerges as if from another world: cobalt blue glaciers, icebergs breaking into alpine lakes and the towering red rock spires of the Fitz Roy Massif all around.

The Chilean side is smaller, narrower, filled with islands and inlets, wild seascapes and rugged coasts. In the North, in the foothills of the Andes, is the Lake District: lilac waters framed by towering snow-capped peaks. In the south, nothing: hundreds of miles of great empty space where only the glittering silence of the true wilderness awaits. There are many national parks in Patagonia, many highlights to see; but there is only one king: Torres del Paine.

Located in the Chilean side of Southern Patagonia, this is the most awe-inspiringly beautiful national park on the continent. The very first tourist here, a British aristocrat by the name of Lady Florence Dixie, who visited in 1889, long before it was a national park, proclaimed: '... now, as if by magic, from the bowels of the earth, a grand and glorious landscape had sprung up around us'. There is something almost surreal, about the scenery here – as if the three jagged knives of the Paine massif that form the centrepiece of the park, those impossibly steep granite towers soaring 6,000 feet upwards from the Patagonian steppe, are actually spires of some great, fallen cathedral, a vast citadel of stone, lost in the embers of time.

Deeper in the park there are enormous blue glaciers pouring imperceptibly slowly into deep turquoise lakes;

Photo: Liam Quinn

ancient forests where red fur guanacos and the imposing rheas, like a curious kind of ostrich, graze the high plains, pumas stalking the shadows behind. Lagoons of lush green reflect the sky in perfect mirror symmetry; giant icebergs, like sparkling sculptures, drift past, close enough to touch. Being here is like looking into a fabled kingdom, a world of dreams, where the beauty of the world is so close, so rich, it's almost a taste, a feeling that seeps inside and stays forever.

But as spectacular as Patagonia, and its king is now, it's about to get even better. Kristine Tompkins, who served as CEO for the global outdoor clothing company, Patagonia, and her late husband Doug Tompkins, who founded The North Face, have recently donated more than a million acres of Patagonian land to the people of Chile – the largest private land donation in history – which will be matched by a further 9 million acres of federal land from the Chilean government. Together they will create a chain of seventeen national parks around Patagonia, one of the largest contiguous protected areas in the world, preserving for all time one of its most stunning places. Torres del Paine may be the king, but an entire kingdom will soon blossom around it.

WHERE: The nearest main town, and transport hub, is Punta Arenas, Chile: *www.parquetorresdelpaine.cl*

DON'T MISS: The 50-mile W Trek, one of the most famous long-distance hikes in the world. Taking in all the main sites of the park, it's possible to stay overnight in a series of mountain refuges along the way, many of which are in gorgeous locations and offer dining rooms, showers and proper beds. Booking ahead is essential. See the park website for details.

TOP TIP: Patagonia has notoriously changeable weather. Make sure to pad your schedule with an extra couple of days to avoid disappointment. The summer months (December–February) have the mildest temperatures, but the strongest winds and the biggest crowds. For many, the shoulder seasons of September, October, November, April and May are a good compromise with fewer tourists, beautiful wildflowers in spring and golden leaves in autumn.

WHILE YOU'RE THERE: Los Glaciares National Park is only a few hours away and should be combined with any visit to Torres del Paine. But keep an eye out for the new Ruta de Los Parques, the 'Route of Parks', too. This roughly 1,500-mile self-drive route, expected to launch in autumn 2018, will take in all the new national parks and conservation land donated by the Tompkinses as well as many of Patagonia's other highlights. Driving it will be the road trip of a lifetime: *www.chile.travel/en*

LOS GLACIARES NATIONAL PARK, ARGENTINA

Glaciers are the sculptors of the planet. These giant rivers of ice flow at imperceptibly slow speeds – most of the time just a few millimetres a day – but they shape the ground beneath them with a force barely rivalled in nature. They are formed over millions of years as fallen snow, instead of melting away piles on top of itself, becoming increasingly compressed and eventually transforming into dense pellets of ice. As these layers get thicker, the ice binds together to form a huge solid mass, which begins to move under its own weight, scouring the land beneath it, crushing, grinding and toppling everything in its path.

At the height of the last Ice Age glaciers covered one third of the Earth's surface. When they finally retreated they left behind the landscape we live in today – glacial valleys and lakes, mountain ridges and moraines, the fertile, mineral-rich soil of the plains. Glaciers are the dynamism of the planet. They exist on every continent of the world. But Los Glaciares National Park, in the far southern reaches of Patagonia, is special, for here, among the rugged foothills and ancient forests of the Andes, are some of the biggest, most accessible and beautiful rivers of ice on Earth.

The centrepiece of the park is the Perito Moreno glacier. Creeping forward at up to six feet per day, it is one of the most active glaciers in the world, an enormous wall of jagged ice, nearly twenty miles long, three miles wide and almost 200 feet high, spilling into the milky blue waters of Lake Argentino. Where the glacier meets the lake, icebergs the size of buildings are calved, or broken off, in thunderous cracks and rushing waves. It's violent, but beautiful too. Hike to the edge of the glacier wall (there are a network of easy to follow catwalks), or take a boat, and you'll see crystalline statues of pale blue icebergs floating downstream; dazzling forms that sparkle in the sunlight like frozen monuments, towering adrift, and yet dwarfed by the vast sheet of ice from which they're born. Join a guided trek on the surface of Perito Moreno itself and you'll feel like you're walking on another planet, a speck of life standing on the white tongue of a gargantuan frozen beast.

There are other glacier stars here too. Upsala, at 336 square miles, is the largest in South America and accessible only by boat – a hair-raising weave between freshly calved icebergs; Spegazzini, a sweep of steep ice, like a colossal frozen fortress; Viedma, curving into the opaque waters of Lake Viedma, snow-capped peaks rising all around. In total, there are 47 major glaciers in the park, as well as more than 200 additional smaller ones dotted in between – a labyrinth of flowing ice and power, casting the Andean valleys in a luminous turquoise and deep blue glow. Feeding it all from above is the vast Southern Patagonian Ice Field, a 5,000-square-mile wilderness of cold and snow where the truly intrepid can still reach unexplored corners in what is one of the last uncharted parts of South America.

Then there are the mountains. The peaks of Los Glaciares National Park are some of the most photogenic in the world, sharp granite towers, 11,000 feet tall, like giant fingers reaching for the sky. At its centre is Mount Fitz Roy, or El Chaltén in native tongue, surrounded on all sides by glorious, steep trails with ever-expanding views unfolding on each bend. The landscape here feels somehow bigger, grander, filled with more drama and life, like walking through an oil painting where the colours have been exaggerated, yet of course, here they haven't. It's real.

But there is something poignant about the park too. Glaciers are the canary in the coalmine of climate change, the sentinels of global warming, and most of them today are in rapid retreat. Upsala alone has receded two miles since 2001, following a worldwide trend that is accelerating at an alarming rate. It's like watching a ticking clock. Melting glaciers, in many parts of the world, will mean rising sea levels, dwindling fresh water supplies and an almost inconceivable loss of human habitat and life. Glaciers may be the sculptors of the Earth, but they can be its destroyer too. It's up to us.

WHERE: Santa Cruz Province, Argentina. The main gateway town is El Calafate: *www.losglaciares.com/en/parque*

Photo: MIKEMDQ

DON'T MISS: Trekking on the Perito Moreno glacier. The views from the surrounding catwalks are immense, the boat will take you even closer, but to actually stand upon the glacier itself, to hear the creek and bellow of the ice moving beneath you, is an adventure few will experience and none will forget. The full day hike must be undertaken with a certified guide. Minimum age is usually ten years old. Numerous operators can be found in the nearby town of El Calafate.

TOP TIP: El Calafate may be the main point of entry, but consider spending a night or two in the village of El Chaltén, Argentina's unofficial capital of trekking, too. Much smaller, and less touristy, this colourful village right at the foot of the stunning Mount Fitz massif, is the perfect base for independent explorations deeper into the park, with numerous world-class trails leaving right from the village itself.

WHILE YOU'RE THERE: Torres del Paine National Park, in Chile (highlighted in the previous chapter) is only a few hours away and should be combined with Los Glaciares on any Patagonian adventure. But make time to explore the hidden corners of the region as well: Perito Moreno National Park (not to be confused with the glacier of the same name), 280 miles to the north, is one of the least known parks in the region, receiving only a few thousand visitors per year, making it an excellent counterpart to the popular Los Glaciares: *www.argentina.travel/en*

IGUAZU NATIONAL PARK, BRAZIL AND ARGENTINA

The Iguazu Falls, on the border of Argentina and Brazil, is the most spectacular waterfall on Earth. There are taller ones: Angel Falls, in Venezuela (also featured in this book) is almost ten times as high; bigger ones: Victoria Falls, on the Zambia–Zimbabwe border, is the largest curtain of falling water on the planet; and more famous ones: Niagara receives at least 10 million more visitors a year. But there are none more beautiful.

Formed from close to 300 individual cascades, pouring down from the upper Iguazu River in an enormous 1.7-mile horseshoe, the first glimpse is a visceral, emotional experience – something sensed with the whole body, not just the eyes. Walls of white thunder plummet hundreds of feet to the ground; the Earth shakes; rainbows are cast in its mist. Surrounded by rainforest on all sides, Iguazu is power and beauty in perfect balance, a screaming vortex of raw kinetic energy exploding from the jungle like a white panther.

In native dialect, the name Iguazu means 'great water'. The Guarani Indians, who were the guardians of the falls prior to the arrival of the Spanish in the 16th century, feared and respected the waterfall as a living deity. Every year they would sacrifice a virgin to the serpent god, M'Boi, who they believed lived in the river. These girls were carefully selected and raised from birth for that sole purpose. But, one day M'Boi got greedy.

Legend has it that a beautiful woman, called Naipi, who was already engaged to her true love, Taruba, was walking beside the river and stopped to look at her reflection in the

Photo: Pedro J Pacheco

water. M'Boi, seeing this, thought she was the most beautiful woman he had ever laid eyes upon and demanded that the Guarani offer her to him instead. But before the elders of the tribe could sacrifice her, Taruba swept her up in his canoe and stole her away. Furious, M'Boi chased them, forcing the Earth to split in their path, creating the Iguazu waterfall and tumbling their canoe over the falls. Taruba was flung to the embankment where M'Boi immediately turned him into a palm tree, overlooking the water's edge; Naipi was trapped in the canoe, but just before she was about to crash he turned her into a rock at the base of the falls. This was M'Boi's jealous revenge, separating the two lovers for all eternity by the waterfall he created, doomed to look forever into each other's eyes and never be able to touch.

Whether you believe the legend or not, a huge rainbow stretches over the falls most days, rising from Naipi's rock on the Argentinian side to a palm tree overlooking the falls on the Brazilian side. Proof, some say, of their enduring love, despite the serpent god's trap.

But deity or not, the Iguazu Falls are powerful indeed. At peak times the flow rate is 450,000 cubic feet per second, enough to fill 300 Olympic size swimming pools every minute. The largest individual fall, and undoubtedly the star attraction, is called Devil's Throat, a vast semi-circular ring of raging white water that plunges 275 feet to a narrow chasm below. Up close, the sound is deafening, almost supernatural in its force. It's like watching an ocean fall off a cliff into an abyss of storm clouds below.

Best of all, Iguazu is still wild. Rainforest surrounds it on all sides; toucans, jaguars, monkeys roam free. In total, there are over 400 species of birds, 80 species of mammal and 2,000 types of plants in the surrounding forests, one of the richest ecosystems on the planet.

Today, the protected area of the falls is actually made up of two separate national parks – Iguaçu National Park on the Brazilian side and Iguazu National Park on the Argentinian. The Argentinian side is larger and, in general, allows closer proximity to the falls with catwalks leading up to the very edge of many individual falls – including the Devil's Throat. The Brazilian side, while more compact, offers broader panoramic views of the area as a whole. Both can, and should, be seen on a single trip.

It's a view you're not likely to forget. Of all the landscapes in the world, from mountains and canyons to beaches and the rugged coast, waterfalls are unique. There is something in the movement, in the natural power and incessant energy that soaks into your soul as much as your skin. All waterfalls are special in their own way, but Iguazu, set deep in the jungle, a bridge between two lost lovers, a falling ocean, wild, raging, power and beauty in perfect balance, is the most spectacular of all.

WHERE: In Brazil, Paraná, 420 miles west of Curitiba (www. visitbrasil.com). The nearest town is Foz do Iguaçu. And in Argentina, Misiones, 800 miles north of Buenos Aires. The nearest town is Puerto Iguazú: *www.argentina.travel*

DON'T MISS: Taking a jet boat to the base of the falls – a drenching cruise, offered on both sides of the border, that provides the closest possible proximity to the waterfall and a soaking wet ride you'll never forget. If you can afford it the Belmond Hotel das Cataratas (*www.belmond.com/hotel-das-cataratas-iguassu-falls*) is the only hotel located in the national park on the Brazilian side, just a few minutes' walk from the falls, and allows access before and after the park officially opens and closes. The Sheraton Iguazu (*www.sheratoniguazu.com*), on the Argentinian side, offers similar deals.

TOP TIP: The falls are at their biggest, and arguably most spectacular, in the rainy season months of December–February. But, January and February are also the most crowded as many locals take their holidays at this time. Excessive rain can close off some of the catwalks at this time as well. March and April may be a good compromise (but avoid Easter at all costs), with less rain, more comfortable temperatures and still relatively high water flow. Avoid weekends.

WHILE YOU'RE THERE: Make sure to experience the rainforest of the surrounding region too – there are a range of excellent ecolodges that offer jungle trekking, bird-watching and more. Look for one that works with members of the Guarani tribe. Your stay will benefit them directly and their insights into the forest, and the falls themselves, will be a highlight of your trip. Yacutinga Lodge is one of the best: *www.yacutinga.com/en/nature-culture.html*

MADIDI NATIONAL PARK, BOLIVIA

The Amazon rainforest is the largest tropical rainforest in the world. Covering 2.1 million square miles of Brazil, Peru, Ecuador, Bolivia, Colombia, Venezuela, Guyana, Suriname and French Guyana – roughly 40 per cent of the entire South American continent – this vast expanse of 400 billion trees is twice as large as the whole of Argentina and twenty times bigger than the UK. If it were a country it would be the ninth largest in the world.

But size is only part of it. Within this enormous swathe of thick, fertile jungle, much of it still unexplored, there exists 10 per cent of the world's known species and one fifth of the planet's freshwater supply. Its trees produce 20 per cent of the world's oxygen.

Then there's the river: stretching 4,080 miles from the tip of the Peruvian Andes to the Atlantic Ocean, the Amazon River is the longest, and most voluminous river system in the world. An astonishing 28 billion gallons of water flow from its mouth into the ocean every minute. In a single day, it could supply all the freshwater needs of New York City for nine years straight.

There are many ways to see this great forest. Brazil, with roughly 60 per cent of the Amazon in its borders, is the most obvious. From the city of Manaus, the main hub, there are riverboat cruises, ecolodges and jungle treks of all varieties and budgets. Yasuni National Park, in Ecuador, is another good option and would make an excellent complement to a Galápagos adventure.

But Madidi National Park, in the north-west corner of Bolivia where the snow-capped peaks of the Andes meet the lush green edge of the Amazon basin, is special. Receiving a fraction of the visitors of the better-known parks of the region, Madidi offers an unfiltered Amazon experience – and one of the most affordable too. Wilderness is paramount. The tourism is sustainable and low-impact, mostly run in conjunction with the local indigenous tribes and benefitting them in the process. This is what the Amazon should be: small footprints and big adventures, the rainforest raw and unfettered from modern needs.

The wildlife is mind-blowing. For a forest twice the size of India, and all of it teeming with amazement, Madidi is,

Photo: Paul B

perhaps, the crown jewel. A recent eighteen-month study of the park's biodiversity revealed that this solitary reserve contains almost half of all the mammals found in the whole of North and South America, as well as a third of all neotropical amphibians and an extraordinary one in five species of birds worldwide.

But that's just scratching the surface: jaguars, sloths, pumas, capybaras, tapirs and monkeys of all kinds call this home; there are manatees and pink river dolphins in the water and harpy eagles, macaws and 60 unique types of hummingbird in the skies. This tiny corner of the Amazon jungle, it turns out, may well contain a greater diversity of life than anywhere else on the planet.

The terrain is just as varied too. The forest is the star, but within its 7,335 square miles are 18,000-foot-tall mountain peaks, permanently shouldered in glaciers and snow, steep cloud forests, open savannah, rolling grasslands, deep tropical lakes and rivers running with thick white water. It's as if all of South America, all the myriad ecosystems of the entire continent, has found a home in this one, solitary park.

But even more wondrous than the wildlife, or the land itself, is the people. Indigenous tribes like the Tacana, Quechua, Araona and more have called these forests home for thousands of years. Their knowledge is unrivalled, an oral library, centuries in the making, filled with secrets we have only just begun to understand. When you come to Madidi, you come to their home. You see the Amazon through their eyes, how they hunt, fish; you learn about their ceremonies, legends and beliefs.

That's important, not just because of the insights it provides us with, but because the true wonder of the Amazon is not what we can see today, but what is still waiting to be discovered. Twenty five per cent of all prescription drugs derive from plants found in rainforests, yet only 1 per cent of tropical plants have been studied for their medicinal properties. We know more about the bottom of the ocean than we do about the canopy of the Amazon rainforest. Right now, in that vast fertile basin there are cures for cancer, AIDS and diseases we haven't even imagined yet, just waiting to be discovered. Chances are, it'll be the indigenous people – many of whom have still never made contact with the outside world – that will show us the way.

Which is exactly what makes national parks, like Madidi, so important. Right now, in the time it's taken you to read this chapter, 500 acres of Amazon rainforest have been cleared. Twenty per cent of the entire forest has been lost to logging, cattle and farming to date. But it's not too late.

The national parks of the Amazon are this great rainforest's last bastion of defence and, just maybe, our last chance at salvation too. There is nowhere more alive, no place more vital for our survival or worthy of our protection than here. The Amazon is more than just a collection of superlatives. It is the lungs of the planet, the medicine cabinet of the world. To be here is to understand in an instant the infinite creativity of evolution, to feel the interconnectedness of all things, and see, with your own eyes, nature at her richest and most fertile. The Amazon is more than just a forest: it's a living monument to life itself and Madidi is her crown jewel.

WHERE:　La Paz Department, North-west Bolivia. The nearest town, and base for the national park, is Rurrenabaque, a short flight from La Paz: *www.bolivia.travel*

DON'T MISS: Seeing the jungle at night – many ecolodges offer night treks as part of their stay, a thrilling experience that showcases a completely different side to the rainforest.

TOP TIP: Stay in an indigenous run ecolodge in the heart of the jungle for the best experience. It won't be luxurious, and you'll need plenty of bug spray, but seeing the jungle through the eyes of the people that live there will be an experience you'll never forget and one that will benefit them at the same time too. Chalalan Ecolodge (*www.chalalan.com*) and Madidi Jungle Ecolodge (*www.madidijungle.com*) are two good options.

WHILE YOU'RE THERE: Make sure to see Bolivia's other natural highlights, including Lake Titicaca, the highest navigable lake in the world and home to the magical floating islands of the Uros people, and the Salar de Uyuni, the largest salt flat on the planet located near the town of Uyuni, in South-western Bolivia: *www.bolivia.travel*

TIKAL NATIONAL PARK, GUATEMALA

The ancient Mayans were one of the world's most extraordinary civilisations. Without advanced tools, or even the wheel, they managed to build enormous cities of stone in the middle of one of the densest jungles on Earth. They developed the first written language of the Americas, an elaborate system of over 800 different symbols and syllables that took almost 200 years to decipher. They mastered advanced farming and irrigation techniques, built complicated looms for weaving cloth and produced the first rubber products in the world, thousands of years before Goodyear patented the process for tyres.

But it's what they managed to achieve in astronomy that really blows your mind. Using only the naked eye astronomer priests were able to predict equinoxes and solstices with a level of accuracy that matches modern science today. They calculated the length of a solar year to be 365.242 days; the current measurement is 365.242198. They were out on the lunar month by less than nine seconds.

Then suddenly, without warning, they were gone. Having thrived in the jungles of what is now Central America for close to 3,000 years, creating one of most advanced civilisations anywhere in the world at the time, by *c.* AD 1200 they had abandoned almost all of their *Tollans*, or principle cities, and disappeared into the jungle forever. What happened to the ancient Mayans remains one of the world's great mysteries – overpopulation, deforestation and severe drought could all be contributing factors. But they didn't leave without a trace.

There are Mayan ruins scattered throughout Central America, some are among the most spectacular archaeological sites in the world. One is Chichén Itzá, in Mexico's northern Yucatán peninsula, whose buildings have been constructed according to precise astronomical measurements. Another is Caracol in Belize, home of Caana, the Sky Palace – a spectacular 140-foot-tall pyramid.

But Tikal is special. Surrounded by jungle, and remote enough to avoid the hordes of tourists that can be found at other archaeological sites in the region, visiting Tikal is like stepping into a lost world. The buildings are shrouded in trees and overgrowth as if born from the jungle floor itself; the forest trails that lead between the main sites are filled with howler monkeys shaking the trees. If you want to do more than just understand the Mayans, if you want to feel the resonance of that once great culture, the echo of their day-to-day life reverberating through the forest still, then it is to Tikal National Park that you must come.

They began settling here, in what is now the Maya Forest

Photo: Arian Zwegers

of Northern Guatemala, around 800 BC and remained until the city was abandoned sometime in the 9th century. What they created in that time is staggering. The central section alone contains over 3,000 individual buildings and covers more than six square miles. But the national park, and the archaeological site it protects, extends far further, a total of 223 square miles in all, creating the largest excavated site on the American continent. And we've only begun to scratch the surface. It is estimated that less than 30 per cent of the total city has been unearthed to date. The rest is lying dormant beneath centuries of overgrowth, shrouded in a blanket of thick green jungle, waiting for its secrets to be revealed.

At the centre of the site is the Great Plaza, a vast courtyard ringed by temples, terraces, palaces and ball-courts (where the Mayans would play a kind of bloody game of basketball, in which the vanquished would lose their lives as well as the game). On one side is the Temple of the Grand Jaguar, a spectacular 144-foot-tall pyramid that rises through nine tiers corresponding to the nine levels of the Mayan underworld; inside is the tomb of Ah Cacau, one of Tikal's greatest rulers, surrounded with precious jade and pearls from the Caribbean coast. Opposite is the equally impressive Temple of the Masks, its steep stairway leading 125 feet up to the best view of the central area, from where you can see the ceremonial areas of the northern and central acropolis, where more temples and residences for the Mayan elite can be found. Carved stelae – pillar-like monoliths commemorating great battles and rulers – are dotted everywhere; and, hidden deep in the jungle, the mysterious Lost World complex of smaller pyramids and buildings, from where it is thought astronomer priests would track the movement of the heavens, calculating with precise detail the best times to plant, harvest and go to war.

But the highlight is the soaring Temple IV, a 213-foot-tall stepped pyramid that rises above the entire site – thought to be the tallest monument ever built by the Mayans. Even now in these times of skyscrapers and impossible buildings it feels unreal; at the time of the Mayans it would have seemed divine. Climb to the top and you will see an endless sea of green, the forest canopy rolling like waves as far as the eye can see, pyramids poking above the trees like enormous stone totems. This was the world the Mayans saw too, unchanged since the foundations of the first temple were laid.

That's what makes Tikal unique: you can still feel it. Here, in this masterpiece of ancient architecture, where one of the world's most remarkable civilisations lived, worshipped and watched the heavens, solving the mysteries of the cosmos with nothing but their intellect and imagination, an echo of their presence remains; here, a part of the ancient Mayans lives on.

WHERE: Petén Province, Northern Guatemala, a one-hour drive from Flores, the nearest city, which also has air connections: *www.visitguatemala.com*
www.tikalnationalpark.org

DON'T MISS: Watching the sunrise from the top of Temple IV, one of the best you'll ever see.

TOP TIP: Stay in one of three small lodges within the national park for early morning access; you'll have the entire park to yourself – perfect for catching the sunrise or sunset (*www.tikalinn.com/en*, *www.jaguartikal.com*, *www.junglelodgetikal.com*). Alternatively, Tikal National Park is on the border with Belize. Basing yourself there, rather than in Guatemala, can be a good option for those who prefer better infrastructure, increased security and higher standards of accommodation. Film director Francis Ford Coppola's boutique jungle hotel, Blancaneaux Lodge, just over the border in Belize, is beautiful, has excellent guides and is only a couple of hours drive from Tikal: *www.thefamilycoppolahideaways.com/en/blancaneaux-lodge*

WHILE YOU'RE THERE: Visit Caracol, another mesmerizing Mayan site – just a short drive from Tikal on the other side of the Belize border: *www.travelbelize.org*

CANAIMA NATIONAL PARK, VENEZUELA

Canaima National Park, deep in the jungle of South-east Venezuela, is home to the tallest waterfall on Earth. Pouring out of an enormous flat-top mesa, or table mountain, called a *tepui* (meaning 'house of the gods' in local dialect), Angel Falls plummets a mind-blowing 3,212 feet to the forest floor, including a spectacular uninterrupted drop of 2,647 feet. Rivals don't even come close to measuring up. Angel Falls is nine times the size of Victoria Falls in Africa; eleven times as high as Iguazu in Brazil and Argentina; and fifteen times loftier than Niagara Falls, in North America. If you were to stand on the tip of the tallest building in the world, the Burj Khalifa in the United Arab Emirates – a skyscraper so elevated it's possible to see the sun set twice in a single day (once from the lower floors and then again from the top), you would still be almost 500 feet short of the summit. Perch yourself on the peak of the Empire State Building and you wouldn't even reach halfway.

The indigenous name for the falls is 'Kerepakupai-Meru', 'the waterfall of the deepest place', which was given to it by the local Pemón people who have inhabited the region for centuries. The name Angel comes from an American aviator, called Jimmie Angel, who discovered the waterfall for Western eyes in 1933 while piloting scouting missions in the region for gold, diamonds and oil. He returned soon after with his wife, and two Venezuelan guides, landing on the top of the tepui near the source of the falls. But disaster struck. Their plane became hopelessly stuck in the mud, forcing them to trek down on foot – a treacherous eleven-day ordeal that, somehow, they all survived. The romance of that extraordinary adventure caught the world's attention and journalists, photographers and scientists soon followed. Angel Falls became a worldwide phenomenon overnight.

But those that came found something equally remarkable here: the tepuis themselves. Covering roughly 65 per cent of the park, these unique geologic formations house one of the most remarkable ecosystems on the planet. Rising straight up from the jungle, with sheer cliffs on all sides like an enormous obelisk, these flat-top table-like mountains, which number over 100 and can reach close to 10,000 feet high, are like little worlds in themselves. Thought to be a remnant of the supercontinent Gondwanaland, the tepuis were pushed skyward when that land mass began to break up, isolating them from the mainland for the last 180 million years. As a result, the ecosystems on the top have evolved in complete isolation from the rest of the world. They are like islands in the sky, each with their own climatic conditions and each housing their own community of plants and animals – many of which are endemic to that one summit alone.

Many are still unexplored too. While a few tepuis can be climbed (though it's not easy – getting to the top of the

Photo: Anagoria

first one took 50 years of exploration), some are simply too difficult to scale, meaning we have absolutely no idea what's up there. When we do finally get a look, it'll be like peering back in time to a glimpse of the planet millions of years ago, a glimpse of prehistoric worlds, never before seen by human eyes.

That's what makes Canaima great: one national park but two wonders of the world. A waterfall so tall, the cascade evaporates to mist before it ever reaches the ground, soaking the land for miles around; and islands in the sky, so isolated that there are creatures we have never even dreamed of living up there, worlds on top of worlds, waiting to be explored. There is something comforting in that. In a planet ever shrinking, where the far reaches of every dark corner can be illuminated by a computer screen, Canaima reminds us that there are still blank spaces on the map, still waterfalls to fly by, adventures to be had. Jimmie would have approved.

WHERE: Gran Sabana region, Bolivar, Venezuela. The nearest town is Canaima: *www.think-venezuela.net*

DON'T MISS: The tepuis. Most people just come to see Angel Falls. If you can afford it, a helicopter ride will show you the tepui summits (some even land on top) as well as offering the most spectacular views of the falls themselves. There are also treks up a few of the more accessible tepuis, the most popular being Roraima, but the walking is strenuous, sustained and only advisable for the seriously fit.

TOP TIP: The flow rate of the falls lessens considerably in the dry season. Come June to September to see it at its best, but be prepared for clouds and delays. Factoring in an extra couple of days, based in the nearby village of Canaima, a delightful spot on the shores of the Canaima Lagoon, will help to avoid disappointment.

WHILE YOU'RE THERE: Spend a few days relaxing in the beautiful Los Roques Archipelago National Park, 80 miles off the coast of Caracas – the point of entry into the country for most international travellers. Featuring some of the most beautiful and pristine beaches and coral reefs in the country this is the perfect complement to a jungle-filled Canaima adventure: *www.losroques.org*

MANÚ NATIONAL PARK, PERU

When the Spanish sacked the Inca city of Cuzco in 1533 they expected to find unimaginable riches of gold and treasure hidden within. But the Inca king, Inkarri, was clever. Knowing the infamous conquistador Pizzaro and his army were closing in on the capital, he moved his treasure deep into the Amazon jungle, concealing it in a secret stronghold that was known only to a select few of his people. That stronghold was called Paititi, 'Home of the Jaguar Father', but we know it by another name: the Lost City of Gold.

Or so the legend goes. Since then, countless treasure hunters, explorers and archaeologists have spent their lives looking for it. None have been successful. But the legend of Paititi, the fabled lost city of the Incas, lives on and the search, to this day, continues. It may be myth, but if it does exist then the experts agree: it's probably somewhere deep in the uncharted jungle of Manú National Park, Peru.

There are a number of reasons why. Stories of a kingdom

Photo: Ludovico Alcorta

hidden where the Andes and the rainforest meet have been passed down through generations of Incan descendents, an oral history that dates back to the time of the conquistadors and points directly to where Manú is located now. Then there's the Pusharo petroglyphs. Discovered in a remote part of the park, in 1921, these strange drawings, etched in stone by an unknown people centuries ago, have yet to be deciphered. The word Pusharo is not known, but it is similar to the Quechua, or Incan, word Pukaro, meaning fortress, leading some scholars to believe they may be a kind of map that, once deciphered, will reveal the location of Paititi.

But perhaps most convincing is a fragment of parchment discovered in 2001, by Italian archaeologist Mario Polia, hidden in the Vatican archives. Written by a missionary named Andres Lopez and dated 1600, the document appears to contain a description of a large city deep in the rainforest, overflowing with gold and treasure, which the natives refer to as Paititi.

Since that discovery efforts have intensified. Most recently expeditions led by French explorer Thierry Jamin have uncovered ancient Inca ruins, hidden throughout the region, leading him to believe they are getting closer. At the time of writing, a curious looking square 'mountain', or physical structure of some kind, completely covered in thick, impassable jungle, was discovered using aerial photography. The local Machiguenga Indians claim that Paititi is on its summit. Jamin and colleagues hope to provide conclusive proof soon.

But, lost city or not, Manú is special for other reasons. Covering 7,200 square miles of South-western Peru, at the meeting point of the tropical Andes and the Amazon Basin, Manú National Park protects one of the most pristine and untouched parts of the Amazon Rainforest. There are no roads in; remoteness (to date) has protected it from logging and drilling. To get here you must endure a ten-hour bus ride on bumpy tracks; or a flight and then a six-hour boat ride down the Manú River. And that's just to the edge; there are vast sections where no one is allowed to go and others that no Western eye has ever seen before. But it's worth the effort. For here is the Amazon at its most abundant, untouched by human hands or greed. There are more than 200 species of mammal, including fourteen individual types of monkey, 800 classes of bird and 68 kinds of reptile making it one of the most biologically rich places on Earth. Everything moves; everything is alive.

Even more impressive, Manú protects an unknown number of indigenous tribes, many of whom still hunt, fish and forage for food as they have done for thousands of years. Some, such as the Machiguengas, are well documented and choose to live in semi-contact with the outside world. Others, like the Amahuacas and Yaminahuas, we only know through reports from other tribes. But there are others still that we have never heard of, men and women that have no knowledge of mobile phones, computers or cars, that know only this forest and nothing of the world around them.

As for lost cities, the Amazon has recently unearthed a surprise. Up until very recently it was assumed that the rainforest was too inhospitable to support an advanced culture – for serious scientists lost cities in the jungle were the stuff of myth and ridicule. But now, barely perceptible but to the trained eye and completely overgrown in jungle, a vast network of Pre-Columbian settlements dating back as far as the 8th Century, has been discovered in a remote and barely charted part of the Brazilian Amazon. Complete with moats, plazas, causeways, bridges, sophisticated housing and more, if verified it would be as advanced as any European city of that time, able to support as many as 60,000 people. Such a discovery would throw out every preconception of the development of humankind we have in the Americas. It would change our ideas of where we come from, how we evolved and what we know. Perhaps Paititi will be found, perhaps it won't. But in the end, the true gold of the Amazon may not be in the treasures it hides, but in the secrets that it reveals about us.

WHERE: Manú and Paucartambo Provinces, Peru. Flights/buses depart from Cuzco: *www.peru.travel*

DON'T MISS: A visit to Lake Otorongo to see the resident family of giant river otters – one of the only places in the world where you can see this remarkable animal.

TOP TIP: The dry season, from May to November, is better for hiking and exploring the park on foot. The wet season, December to April, can be better for spotting wildlife but expect more mosquitoes and lots of rain. The remote Manú Wildlife Centre is one of the best places to stay with over 30 miles of well-managed trails and excellent wildlife viewing, including the best odds of spotting a jaguar anywhere in the park.

WHILE YOU'RE THERE: Combine a trip to Manú National Park with some of Peru's other legendary Inca highlights, the ancient city of Cuzco, the Sacred Valley of the Incas and the incredible fortress complex of Machu Picchu are just a few: *www.peru.travel*

SIERRA NEVADA DE SANTA MARTA NATIONAL NATURAL PARK, COLOMBIA

In 1990, the Kogi Indians, who had lived for centuries in complete isolation in the Sierra Nevada Mountains of Northeastern Colombia, decided to make contact with the outside world. They wanted to deliver a message, to let us know that we are damaging the planet (they thought we hadn't realised) and warned that should their mountain home be decimated by our actions, the Earth would soon follow.

It turns out they may be right: their mountain really is vital to the survival of the planet. A landmark study, published in the academic journal, *Science*, in 2013, analysed data from 173,000 protected reserves around the globe, containing more than 21,500 species, in order to assess the location of the most biologically important areas on the planet; those places that house the most threatened species and, if lost, will never be replaced again. Colombia's Sierra Nevada de Santa Marta National Natural Park, the ancestral home of the Kogis, tops that list.

The reason has to do with its location. The Sierra Nevada Mountains are the tallest coastal range in the world, rising from the Caribbean Sea to close to 19,000 feet in less than 30 miles. Such diverse topography has created a huge range of habitats from tropical lowlands and mangrove swamps through cloud forests and arid plains to peaks permanently covered in ice and snow. Every climatic condition on Earth is represented in this singular stone pyramid of a mountain. And because of its unique ecological structure, scientists now agree: what happens here is like a mirror to the rest of the world. The Kogi were right: bad news for them is bad news for us too.

Photo: Colombiaamazinglandscapes

Within these myriad ecosystems are vast numbers of endemic species as well as the most fragile concentration of threatened mammals, birds and amphibians on the planet. Jaguars, tapirs, pumas and bears roam these jungles, condors soar the jagged peaks above; sixteen rivers flow down and irrigate the land for hundreds of miles; there are waterfalls, swimming holes, mist, like breath, rising through the forest all around. Here all the beauty and rich diversity of the Americas is wrapped in 1,500 square miles of irreplaceable habitat, a paradise where the mountains fall swiftly to the sea.

But the highlight is the Lost City. The Kogis are direct descendents of the indigenous Tairona people, who flourished in the region between the 2nd and 16th centuries – one of the few tribes to resist being conquered by the Spanish. The Lost City, Teyuna as it's known locally, was built by them *c.* AD 800 – some 600 years before Machu Picchu – and was only discovered by the outside world in 1975 by local looters. It is, undoubtedly, one of South America's greatest archaeological finds, but it takes some work to see it: there are no easy ways in, only a hard 29-mile round trip hike through steep, inhospitable jungle, camping out along the way.

But it's worth the effort. Spread out over 150 acres of high jungle, overlooking lush rolling mountains on all sides, the site contains a series of circular stone terraces, connected by pebble pathways and rocky steps, that were believed to be the foundations of a once elaborate city. At its peak, Teyuna would have housed as many as 3,000 people and likely functioned as a place of key economic and cultural importance. For the Kogi today, it is a sacred place, known to them as the 'origin of the people from the Earth'. It feels like that too – the centre of one of the most fertile and precious landscapes on the planet, a jungle oasis where the world seems more mystical, mysterious and alive.

But to truly appreciate Teyuna you have to understand the Kogi's cosmology; you have to understand Aluna. For the Kogi, the material world is embedded in thought. Aluna is the term they use for a kind of universal consciousness that underpins all reality. For the Kogi, the world of things outside of us is inseparable from the world of thoughts within.

One consequence of Aluna is that the Earth itself has awareness. The planet is a living, thinking being. The Kogi believe their shamans, known as Mamas, are able to connect to Aluna through a kind of concentrated thought or meditation, which enables them to communicate directly with the planet, helping to maintain its natural order. They see themselves as a conduit between the consciousness of the planet and all living things on it. They call themselves the Elder Brothers for this reason. They protect an ancient wisdom, once shared throughout humanity, that we in the industrialised nations, the Younger Brothers, have now forgotten. That was why they came out of hiding. To remind us that the planet is alive, that we are hurting it, and hurting their mountain too.

That's what makes this park one of the greatest in the world. Because for all its natural wonder and biological importance, its most precious treasure is still the people that live here – about 30,000 in total, including the Kogi and other indigenous descendents of the Tairona. Come and you will hike their paths, see their villages, smile as they pass – bare feet, adorned in all-white robes. The Sierra Nevada de Santa Marta range is more than a national park; it's a gateway to a new way of seeing the Earth, not as an inanimate object, but a living entity. If we can do that, the Kogi say, then we can save their mountain and, just maybe, ourselves too. Perhaps then, we – the Younger Brothers - will have finally grown up.

WHERE: Cesar, Colombia. The beach town of Palomino is often used as a base for the Lost City trek: *www.parquesnacionales.gov.co/portal/en/ecotourism/caribbean-region/sierra-nevada-de-santa-marta-national-natural-park/*

DON'T MISS: The Lost City trek. Various tours are offered for the 28-mile hike, which usually lasts between three and five days depending on how hard you want to go. All visitors must travel with a licensed group. Choose one that has a Kogi, or other indigenous guide for the best experience.

TOP TIP: Watch *From the Heart of the World: the Elder Brothers' Warning*, a documentary about the Kogi's initial contact with the outside world; and *Aluna*, the 2013 follow-up, for an inside look at their culture, beliefs and unique way of life. To find out more about the films and how to support the Kogi, visit: *www.tairona.myzen.co.uk*

WHILE YOU'RE THERE: Spend a few days relaxing on the nearby beaches of Tayrona National Park – pristine white sand kissed by jungle and snow-capped peaks behind. Avoid high season December to February: *www.parquesnacionales. gov.co/portal/en/ecotourism/caribbean-region/tayrona-national-natural-park/*

EUROPE

CAIRNGORMS NATIONAL PARK, SCOTLAND

The Cairngorms National Park is a living landscape. Poets, warriors and queens have walked here; blood has been spilt on this ground. From the primeval forests of Caledonia, that once covered this nation from coast to coast, ancient castles still rise, the land is still tended by crofters who graze their sheep and Highland cattle still work the soil, as they have done for centuries. In winter, snow dusts the ragged peaks: barren granite, grey, white and cold; in summer, colour races through the glens, purple sheaths of thistle and heather, like slicks of paint, too bright to be real. The Cairngorms National Park, in the highlands of Scotland, are storms and silence, dark lashings of rain and shards of iridescent light, like spotlights through the clouds. These hills are the soul of the Scots, the pride of the country, a land soaked in whisky, history and myth.

But though the hills and history may be old, the park itself is relatively new. Formed in 2003, it is the largest national park in the UK – 1,500 square miles of ancient woodlands and lush craggy peaks. The centrepiece is the Cairngorm mountain range itself, home to over 50 Munros – the local term for summits over 3,000 feet – including four of Scotland's five highest peaks. Here, on the top of the country, sub-arctic tundra and frosty windswept crags sweep across the barren mountain slopes. Rolling hills, lush and brazen with colour, spread out as far as the eye can see. And far

Photo: Daniël Hartog

below, the dark eyes of icy lochs puncture the Earth, deep blue and crystal clear where, just maybe, the monsters of old myths lurk hidden within.

There are many special spots: Ben Macdui, the tallest mountain in the Cairngorms, at 4,295 feet, and the second tallest in the UK (after Ben Nevis, 50 miles to the west); the seven peaks of the Lairig Ghru, probably the most spectacular high mountain pass in the country; Cairngorm Mountain itself, 4,084 feet high with dazzling views on all sides, and a funicular railway that will get you to all but the last 150 feet. And, of course, Lochnagar, the most famous of all the mountains here, immortalised by Lord Byron in his 1807 poem *Lachin Y Gair:*

Yet, Caledonia, belov'd are thy mountains,
Round their white summits though elements war;
Though cataracts foam 'stead of smooth-flowing fountains,
I sigh for the valley of dark Loch na Garr.

Each of these hills, these steep river valleys, peatlands and moors, have a story to tell. The Picts, a fierce and ancient people, who painted their faces blue and defied all conquerors, even the Romans, left behind prehistoric burial mounds and stone circles that date back nearly 6,000 years. The clans who ruled the land from father to son, from the 10th to the 18th century, made their last stand here, at the battle of Culloden in 1746, 3,000 men and boys slaughtered so that Scotland could be subjugated to the crown. Balmoral Castle, where the British Queen and her family still holiday today, is also found in the park. There are old smugglers, trails to hike and paths that follow in the footsteps of drovers, shepherds that would walk their flocks over the hills to market or pasture. The history here isn't something learnt, it's felt in every stone and glen.

Walking is, by far, the most popular activity with hundreds of miles of trails to wander and many more adventures to be had rambling on unmarked hillsides. But there's much else here too. Canoeing is popular, especially down the River Spey, as is fishing with some of the most abundant trout and salmon in Europe in these waters. There is a stunning scenic drive through the high country, called the Snow Roads Scenic Route, which links together three of the Cairngorms' most picturesque villages with many of its natural highlights. Wildlife is everywhere: golden eagles coil on thermals; stags roam the hillsides; there's even Britain's only herd of wild reindeer roaming free among the glens. And there's plenty of whisky too: the Glenlivet Distillery, near the small town of Ballindalloch, which has been perfecting the art since 1824, and the Royal Lochnagar Distillery, near Balmoral, once a favourite of Queen Victoria's, are two of the best. Both offer excellent tastings and tours.

But, in the end, it's the people that make it. The Cairngorms may be the soul of the Scots, but the Scots are the soul of the Cairngorms too. There's never a pub too far away, a friendly dram by the fire, music and laughter. The highlands of Scotland aren't so much a place as a welcome, a sense of belonging, wherever you're from. This land is alive and it breathes life into you too.

WHERE: North-east Scotland, just south of Inverness. The main town within the park is Aviemore: *www.cairngorms.co.uk*

DON'T MISS: 'Bagging a Munro', climbing to the top of one of the park's 52 mountains over 3,000 feet is a must, but if you have time consider walking the long-distance Speyside Way hiking path too. This 65-mile trail follows the valley of the River Spey all the way from the east coast to Aviemore, in the heart of the national park. Even better it can be walked pub-to-pub; a great introduction to the region, with wonderful views and excellent whisky throughout. Allow four–five days for the trip: *www.walkhighlands.co.uk/speyside-way.shtml*

TOP TIP: Time your visit with the Highland Games, a traditional celebration that dates back to the clan era when chieftains would hold sporting contests to choose their strongest warriors. The village of Braemar, which is located inside the national park itself, hosts one of the best gatherings, held on the first Saturday of September each year: *www.visitcairngorms.com/highlandgames*

WHILE YOU'RE THERE: Stop by Scotland's other national park, Loch Lomond and The Trossachs, near Glasgow – one of the UK's most beautiful lakes and the gateway to Scotland's spectacular west coast: *www.lochlomond-trossachs.org*

CINQUE TERRE NATIONAL PARK, ITALY

The Cinque Terre is a park for lovers, artists and anyone that appreciates delicious food and a chilled glass of wine, as much as a jaw-dropping view. Meaning 'five lands' in direct translation, this tiny national park (Italy's smallest at just 15 square miles) on the Ligurian coast, is composed of five historic and pedestrianised villages. Each one is dyed in bright pastels of orange, pink, lilac and yellow, as if drawn straight from an Impressionist's palette, and each tumbles from the lush greenery of the mountains above, down steep terraced slopes, to the dazzle of the deep blue Mediterranean Sea.

There is something magic here, in the Italian Riviera, something in the harmony of architecture and the natural world, in the creations of man and the colours of the Earth, that is rarely seen. The Cinque Terre is art transformed to a living scale, a landscape where the beauty of the world has been enhanced by the people in it, not diminished; where both have been made greater together, as a whole, than either could ever have been on their own.

Each of the five towns has its own distinctive character. The furthest south is Riomaggiore, the oldest of the settlements. Known to have existed as early as the 11th century, tall deep red and ochre houses frame a narrow V-shaped bay, filled with fishermen hauling their nets to shore, a maze of narrow cobbled streets and steep back alleys inside. To the north is Manarola, built in the 12th century and widely recognised as one of the most beautiful villages in Italy. Bright peach and lilac houses dangle from a rocky promontory out to sea. Next is Corniglia, the smallest and quietest of the quintet, perched on a cliff-edge 300 feet above the ocean. Climb to the hilltop here for one of the most breathtaking views of the entire region – 180 degrees of pure azure water in front and the soft coves and inlets of the coast fading to the horizon on either side. Monterosa is the furthest north, livelier than the rest, with the best beach and a historical centre filled with pastel-coloured houses and artisan shops. But the pearl of the park is Vernazza. Historically, this was the only village in the region with a deep harbour, meaning it was also the most prosperous and powerful. Today, that former wealth is reflected in elaborate arcades, archways, balconies and piazzas – like a little Venice. There is a good, sandy beach surrounded by rows of tiny colourful fishing boats and a castle, built over a thousand years ago to defend against Saracen and pirate attacks, looking out across the turquoise waters of the bay.

Photo: CCCP

Even better is what's around them. Each hamlet is connected by a series of walking paths, the most popular of which is the Sentiero Azzurro, or Blue Trail, an eight-mile hiking route that meanders precipitously along the coast, often perched hundreds of feet above the warm lap of the ocean, nothing but sun and sparkle all around. Other paths lead upward to ancient monasteries or wind through Sciacchetrà vineyards, a local wine and speciality of the region, particularly good when paired with fresh basil pesto.

Surrounding them, spilling down the steep mountain slopes like a giant's staircase, are a series of terraces, called *ciàn*, supported by hand-crafted dry-stone walls cut painstakingly into the hillsides over centuries. In total, these primitive walls, which enabled the villagers to thrive despite the precipitous slopes on which they had to farm, cover more than 8 million cubic metres of the region. Stretch them out side by side and they would reach over 4,000 miles – far enough, just about, to cross the Atlantic. Thanks to them, olive groves, lemon trees (for the famous Limoncino aperitif) and vineyards fill the foothills with colour; delicate aromas and the promise of fresh, home-cooked meals soften every step.

And that's the thing. There are few national parks that will feed you this well. Fresh baked mussels stuffed with parmesan and herbs, fried anchovies (caught the traditional way using nets and then salted by hand – a local delicacy), grilled fish stewed in lemon and served on grapevine leaves, seafood carpaccio with spaghetti drizzled in homemade olive oil, fresh pastries baked with chestnuts and raisins, sweet cold gelatos, the best ice cream in the world, eaten while dangling your feet off the dock into the warm waters of the bay. Ligurian cooking is about simplicity, recipes passed down and perfected through generations.

Lovers of food, of art, of history and of each other can all revel in this park. But the greatest love affair here, perhaps, is between the creations of man and nature herself. There are few places where the natural world and the architecture of humankind blend so seamlessly. Perhaps, that's its allure – here we got it right; its magic is its harmony, its perfect balance of colour, culture, taste and life.

WHERE: Liguria, Northern Italy. Take the train to La Spezia, on the Pisa-Genoa line, for connections to all five Cinque Terre villages: *www.parconazionale5terre.it*

DON'T MISS: Walking the Sentiero Azzurro, or Blue Trail, along the coast, which connects all five villages. Although it can be walked in a single day (plan for eight hours of solid hiking) much better is to break it up into smaller sections. A morning walk, followed by a long lunch in a new town, with time to explore afterwards, is the perfect Cinque Terre day.

TOP TIP: Avoid the crowds of summer and come May to early June or September instead – the weather is just as nice and the crowds a fraction as big. For quieter trails, head into the mountains – they're more challenging, but the views are breathtaking and you'll have them all to yourself.

WHILE YOU'RE THERE: Spend a few days (or as long as possible) exploring Florence and the gorgeous Tuscan countryside – just a couple of hours drive east of Cinque Terre National Park. One of the most beautiful regions of Italy, Tuscany is a paradise of soft rolling hills, historic hill top towns and some of the best wine you'll ever drink: *www.visittuscany.com*

MOUNT OLYMPUS NATIONAL PARK, GREECE

According to Homer's epic poem, 'The Iliad', it is in 'the mysterious folds of Olympus', the dark ravines that cut into the jagged hillsides, where the twelve gods of ancient Greece live. On the highest peak, then called the Pantheon, now known as Mytikas, the tallest point in the country at 9,570 feet, sits the throne of Zeus himself, the king of the gods. From here, in his golden courtyard, all the deities of the earth, air and sea would gather and preside over the plight of man.

Olympus was the centre of the ancient Greek universe, glorified in the work of Plato, Sophocles, Hesiod and more. Legends were born here that live on to this day. The ancient Greeks, that great, enlightened civilisation, left us many things: the foundations of democracy and Western philosophic thought; vast leaps in the arts, mathematics and science; they brought us theatre, the Olympic games and some of the most dazzling works of architecture the world has ever seen. Our civilisation today would be unrecognisable if not for the foundations they laid. But their lasting monuments are not so much the ruins they left behind, as the ideas they spawned; and that begins here, on the slopes of fabled Mount Olympus.

The park itself protects all 52 peaks of the Olympus range, comprising a total of 92 square miles of North-eastern Greece. Swift elevation change, and proximity to the Aegean Sea, has created enormous diversity: chamois, wolves and wild boar roam the mountain slopes, along with over 100 species of birds and the famous Greek butterflies, which appear in staggering abundance, filling the mountains with colour.

The hiking is spectacular, with the opportunity to scale the very throne of Zeus itself – a full day's hard walk through lowland oaks and strawberry trees to forests of ancient beech and the bare rock summits of the high mountain tops. Almost as good are the walks through the canyons, particularly the spectacular Epineas Gorge, overlooked by the stone cloisters and domed towers of the mid-16th-century monastery, Agios Dionysus.

Just as rewarding, for many, is the chance to visit traditional villages that surround the mountain: Petra, with breathtaking views of the Pieria Plains; Karya, believed to be the birthplace of the legendary musician Orpheus, who was said to be able to make even the trees and rocks around him dance; Palaios Panteleimonas, a beautifully restored 14th-century village overlooking the Gulf of Thermaikos and the medieval castle, Platamonas. Here, in these rural hamlets, away from the tourist resorts of the coast and the bustle of Athens, it's possible to experience an authentic Greek way of life that has changed little in centuries.

Unsurprisingly, the park is rich in archaeological history too. On the rounded summit of Agios Antonios, south of Mytikas, an open-air sanctuary has been uncovered, dating back more than 2,000 years, to the Hellenistic period. This, it is thought, is the famed Temple of Olympian Zeus, where texts from the 2nd century speak of processions of animals led here each year to make sacrifices to the king of the gods, his share of the meat burnt in an altar fire and placed in a sacred pile of ash on the mountain's edge. Nearby is the chapel of the Prophet Elias, built in the 16th century at a height of 9,196 feet – still, to this day, the most elevated chapel in the Orthodox world, peering over a sea of clouds to snow-capped peaks in the distance below.

But the highlight is the ancient village of Dion. In the

4th century BC this was the holy city of the Macedonians. King Archelaus held nine days of games here, to honour Zeus and his muses. Alexander the Great stopped by on his way to conquer the Persians, sacrificing animals at the Temple of Zeus for good luck, and then donating a statue of his fallen troops on his victorious return. The site features two ancient theatres, one Greek, the other Roman, dating back to its time as a colony of that other great empire, as well as Roman baths, the elaborate Villa of Dionysus, with its intricate mosaic depicting the god riding his chariot, and the spectacular flooded sanctuary of the Egyptian goddess Isis.

Mount Olympus is more than a national park, it is a divine wilderness, a land imbued with history and myth, where the memory of faded deities echoes through these jagged peaks still. Being here it's easy to feel that ancient culture embedded in every stone, to feel the spirit of Zeus himself, as you stand on top of the world and walk in the abode of the gods.

WHERE: Piera and Thessaly regions, North-east Greece. The main village, at the base of Mount Olympus, is Litochoro: *www.olympusfd.gr*

DON'T MISS: Getting down the mountain the fun way. Canyoning is the slightly crazy sport of jumping, abseiling and swimming down rushing mountain gorges and rivers; and Mount Olympus National Park happens to be one of the best places in Europe to try it. Numerous operators offer a range of trips, usually lasting between four to six hours, from family-friendly paddles to extreme white-water adventures.

TOP TIP: Spend at least one night on the mountain. There are nine refuges, many sleeping dozens of people with kitchens and restaurants inside. Refuge C, or Christos Kakkalos Refuge, located 9,000 feet up at the edge of Mouson Plateau and Refuge D, otherwise known as Stavros Refuge or Dimitrios Boundolas Refuge, with its views across the Pieria Plain, are two of the best. Book in advance and as early as possible: *www.olympusfd.gr/us/Katafygia.asp*

WHILE YOU'RE THERE: The Acropolis and Pantheon in Athens, the gateway into Greece for most people, is, of course, a must – but make time for the Oracle of Delphi at the foot of Mount Parnassos, as well. Just two hours west of the capital, it was the ancient Greek's window into the will of the gods and one of the country's most stunning monuments today: *www.thisisathens.org, http://odysseus.culture.gr*

MERCANTOUR NATIONAL PARK, FRANCE

There are many places in the world with beautiful mountains and warm turquoise seas; many places filled with history, art, gastronomy and culture. But few have them all in one place, and none do it with such *savoir faire*. The South of France covers a wide region, from the Alps to the Mediterranean, the glamour of the French Riviera to the lush farmlands of the interior. But its belle, its enchantress, will forever be Provence.

This small corner, in the south-east of the country, has inspired poets, lovers and artists for centuries. It gave the world impressionism; Cézanne, Van Gogh, Gauguin and Matisse all created masterpieces here. The sun shines 320 days a year. Fields of purple lavender brighten the countryside; medieval villages perch on the hills. There

is style and fashion on the coast, the most beautiful and glamorous people in the world, and farming in the foothills that has changed little in centuries. Delicious aromas drift over the land like a warm summer breeze; a drop of chilled wine is never far from hand. Time slows; cares fade. Provence isn't a destination, it's a way of life.

At its heart, on the Italian border, where the Alps meet the hinterland of the French Riviera, is Mercantour National Park, 268 square miles of high mountain scenery and rural French bliss. Six perfect valleys emanate from its central massif, sharp angular peaks that reach over 10,000 feet and can be seen from the ocean, sugar-coated for much of the year in thick dustings of snow. Most of it is uninhabited, a wilderness of impossibly steep gorges, alpine lakes and meadows gleaming with wildflowers: snow-white edelweiss and striking blue gentian – more than 2,000 species in all.

Here, the ferocity of the Alps has been sedated by the south. Lazy paths meander along old shepherd trails through olive groves and forests of larch and spruce. Cows and goats graze languidly in the foothills, their masters, the *vachers*, gathering milk and heating it over wood fires, a technique passed down through generations, to produce some of the world's most delicious cheeses. Beekeepers tend hives nearby, selling pots of fresh honey at weekend markets; chamois skip from rock to rock. Even the waterfalls appear to pause as they slip down craggy slopes, turning to rushing streams filled with wild trout, fresh for the catch.

For the more adventurous, the park is a paradise. Rock climbing and mountaineering, especially in the searing cliffs of La Colmiane and the gorges of Verdon nearby, is incredibly popular. Hikers can head into the high country and never come down for 375 miles, following trails through some of the park's most spectacular mountain scenery. In summer there is mountain biking, para-gliding, canyoning, canoeing, white water rafting and more. In winter, the snowshoeing and cross-country skiing is sublime: nothing but pure white silence, miles away from the chatter of France's famous resorts nearby.

But perhaps most special of all is the history. Twenty eight traditional mountain villages are set within the park's boundaries, many spilling over steep hillsides or perched spectacularly above cliffs and rocky outcrops. The medieval village of Saorge is spread out like an amphitheatre across the high valley, narrow cobbled streets leading to 15th-century stone houses, the baroque-style Franciscan Monastery, filled with colourful frescoes within; Colmars-les-Alpes, in the upper reaches of the Verdon valley, is ringed by stone ramparts and guarded by two 17th-century forts. Châteauneuf d'Entraunes, with its 360-degree views across the Var valley; peaceful Fontan, by the rushing banks of the Roya River. One of the great joys of Mercantour is simply walking between the villages, stopping for plates of freshly made cheese, a glass of wine and a wander in between.

Even better is the chance to explore the rock art of the Vallée des Merveilles, the aptly named Valley of Marvels, where close to 40,000 Bronze Age petroglyphs are carved into the base of Mont Bego. These 3,000-year-old drawings of horned animals, axes, daggers, geometric shapes and human forms represent the largest cache of prehistoric art in Europe – and one of the most visually arresting too.

But don't stop there. To the south, less than an hour away, is the Côte D'Azur: Cannes, Nice, St Tropez, the most glamorous coastline in the world. To the west, the Luberon Valley, one of Provence's most breathtakingly beautiful regions. Italy is just a few miles to the east; some of the country's finest skiing and high alpine scenery, including its largest national park, Vanoise, is less than three hours north. The South of France is special: a way of life, a place where time slows, history lives and the mountains tumble to the sea.

WHERE: Alpes-Maritimes and Alpes-de-Haute-Provence departments, Southern France. The delightful village of Saint-Martin-Vésubie is a good gateway town for the park: *www.france.fr*
www.mercantour.eu

DON'T MISS: Walking the traditional French way, village to village with your very own donkey to carry your bags and lead the way. There are various operators offering anything from day trips to week-long adventures. Itinerance is one of the most popular: *www.itinerance.net*

TOP TIP: Book a local guide to see the prehistoric rock art of the Vallée des Merveilles. They know the best spots, which can be hard to find, and will help make the history of the region come alive. Guides des Merveilles are specialists to the region: *www.guidesdesmerveilles.com*

WHILE YOU'RE THERE: Make sure to visit Vanoise National Park, just a short drive away. France's first and largest national park with stunning high Alpine scenery, wonderful hiking in summer and some of Europe's best skiing in winter: *www.france.fr*

LAKE DISTRICT NATIONAL PARK, ENGLAND

While out walking in the Lake District one stormy day, the 19th-century English poet, William Wordsworth, came across a field of daffodils and wrote these words:

I wandered lonely as a cloud
That floats on high o'er vales and hills,
When all at once I saw a crowd,
A host, of golden daffodils.

That poem, published first in 1807, of which these lines form the opening stanza, has become one of England's most cherished literary works. It defines the spirit of the Lake District; that deep connection to the land, the vast emptiness and rich colour of these rolling valleys and dark, sparkling waters.

The Lake District, in the far North-west corner of England, is the country's most prized national park, a living landscape filled with history, poetry and endless rolling summits to explore. It has inspired countless artists, writers, kings and queens, but it belongs to only one man. The Lake District will forever be Wordsworth's country.

There are sixteen principal lakes in the park, often referred to locally as waters, tarns or meres, each with their own distinctive character. In the south, Windermere is both the park's and England's largest lake, and many people's first port of call: sailing, canoeing and pleasure cruises on the water; huge Victorian mansions lining the shore. To the north, by the village of Ambleside, is Stock Ghyll Force, one of England's most beloved waterfalls and a favourite spot of

Photo: Margo Brodowicz

the poet John Keats, who said of it: 'I shall learn poetry here and shall henceforth write more than ever.'

Nearby is Coniston Water, the setting for another famous literary resident, Arthur Ransome's, classic children's book *Swallows and Amazons.* To the east is Ullswater, where, it is believed, Wordsworth first discovered his crowd of golden daffodils. Steamboats puffing across the water since 1849, it is surrounded by lush farmlands and distant peaks all around.

But perhaps best of all are the quieter corners, where the poetry of the land can still be felt: Buttermere; peaceful and serene, ringed by soft hills and sandy beaches – perfect for picnics and snoozing off the cares of the day. Derwentwater; snow-capped fells, the land ablaze with purples and orange each autumn. Grasmere; nestled at the foot of high rolling fells, where Wordsworth himself lived for nine years and called it: 'The loveliest spot that man hath ever found.'

The walking is superb just about everywhere, but there are a few special routes. Scafell Pike, at 3,209 feet, is England's tallest peak, wild vistas of the Wasdale Valley spreading out from the summit; The Old Man of Coniston, one of the park's most iconic fells; the spectacular Helvellyn, reached by the razor-edge Striding Edge, nothing but hundreds of feet of pure lake air on all sides.

History is never far away either. The Langdale Pikes were home to a Neolithic axe factory where local tribesmen chipped blades from blocks of stone, a highly sought-after tool and weapon that was traded throughout Britain and Ireland. Later, in the Early Bronze Age, nearly 5,000 years ago, the residents of the Lakes built stone circles, smaller versions of Stonehenge – but just as mysterious. Castlerigg, with its 38 primary stones, some as much as ten feet tall, and the 55-stone Swinside Circle, are two of the best. Later still, from around 55 BC to AD 410 the Romans settled here, buttressing up against Hadrian's Wall 40 miles to the north, the frontier of their empire.

Much of the history is still alive too. Cumberland and Westmorland wrestling, introduced by the Vikings, is still practised to this day. Hound Trailing, an 18th-century sport unique to the region, in which specially trained hound dogs race over the fells, following a scented aniseed trail, has been a part of Lake District life for over 200 years. There's even an annual World Gurning Championship. Established in 1267, this ancient fair celebrates the art of pulling a funny face, with prizes awarded for the most grotesque expressions.

Wordsworth wasn't the only literary great to put the Lake District on the map. The other two 'Lake Poets', as they're known, are Samuel Taylor Coleridge, one of the most influential poets of the Romantic period, and Robert Southey, Poet Laureate of England for 30 years – both compatriots and walking companions of Wordsworth himself. But it's Beatrix Potter that steals the show. The beloved author of Peter Rabbit and Jemima Puddle-Duck summered here in the late 1800s with her family, staying in the gothic mansion Wray Castle on the shores of Lake Windermere as well as in properties on Derwentwater and the surrounding area. It was, perhaps, the greatest inspiration of her life and featured heavily in her work. After she found success, she bought farms and land across the Lakes, raised flocks of Herdwick sheep, a breed native to the area, and eventually donated the vast majority of her property to the National Trust for all to cherish and enjoy as she did.

Literary pedigree may have put the Lake District on the map, but Wordsworth worried that growing tourism in the Lakes would somehow diminish that deep serenity he felt watching the daffodils dancing in the breeze. But he needn't have been concerned. Those quiet corners are still here.

That drama of light and storm, of rain clouds and sunbeams, that has inspired authors and artists for centuries, plays on. Lonely clouds racing the high fells, mist rising from the water. The Lake District is poetry still.

WHERE: Cumbria, North-west England. There are numerous gateway towns and villages in the park, depending on where you want to explore. See website for details: *www.lakedistrict.gov.uk*

DON'T MISS: Trying out some of the Lake District's local delicacies: Cumberland sausage with mash and gravy, damson wine, sticky toffee pudding (which was invented here) and, of course, the legendary Kendal Mint Cake – no fells walk would be the same without it.

TOP TIP: Buy Wainwright's *Illustrated Guides to the Lake District Fells*. Not only does it feature some of the best hikes in the park, it also contains the legendary Lake District artist's hand-drawn sketches and writing – a unique insight to the region, from one of its most celebrated residents.

WHILE YOU'RE THERE: Combine your visit with a day or two at the Yorkshire Dales National Park, just a few miles to the east – beautiful rolling green moors, filled with history and the iconic Yorkshire Three Peaks, one of the best hikes in the North of England: *www.yorkshiredales.org.uk*

TRIGLAV NATIONAL PARK, SLOVENIA

The Julian Alps, in Northern Slovenia, may not to be the most well-known part of the Alps, that great mountain chain which covers 80,000 square miles of Europe and stretches all the way from the Mediterranean to the eastern edge of Austria. But they are, perhaps, the most beautiful.

For the locals, that's no secret. Triglav National Park, the crown jewel of the Julian Alps, is one of the most cherished parts of their country, a wonderland of soaring ridges and pyramidal peaks, where it is said you are not a true Slovenian until you have stood upon its highest summit, the 9,396-foot-high, spectacular Mount Triglav itself.

But for many this part of southern central Europe is still undiscovered. Not for long. Here, right on the border of Austria and Italy, in these 340 square miles of pristine wilderness, are the Alps at their most awe-inspiring and sublime. Steep mountain crests rise upwards, dusted in snow; alpine meadows are carpeted in wildflowers where chamois and red deer run free; there are rivers rushing with rapids and deep cobalt lakes, with water as soft as silk. If you are looking for adventure, to experience a part of that great range where precious few outside of the country have trod, then the Julian Alps of Triglav National Park is the place for you.

There are many highlights. Lake Bohinj is the largest lake in the country, surrounded by towering limestone peaks, perfect for summer swims or forest hikes around its shore. Nearby the village of Bohinj is filled with traditional wooden cottages – open haylofts, cow bells ringing as cattle graze the lush mountain slopes, like an alpine fairy

Photo: Tiia Monto

tale made real. Further into the park's southern tip, the Tolmin Gorge rushes with pure emerald water, just a few feet wide but with 180-foot-tall forested cliffs on either side, wooden walkways and hanging bridges meandering in between, like an enchanted kingdom. And, of course, the three-headed massif of Mount Triglav itself: it's a hard seven-hour climb to the top, but on well-marked trails, and the views, stretching all the way to Austria in the north and the Adriatic Sea in the south, are worth the sweat. Few places pack so much variety into a single park; this is the complete mountain topography, a panorama of every imaginable landscape of the Alps; new scenes of awe and wonder unfurling on every bend.

Just as important is the Slovenian culture. Once a part of the former Yugoslavia, the independent country of Slovenia is young, established in 1991, but progressive – fourth out of 180 nations in environmental performance with more than half of its land made up of protected reserves. The people are adventurous and fun – especially if some of the locally-made wine is involved (Slovenia is one of the oldest wine-producing nations in the world). Organic farms and homesteads surround the park, the smell of traditional beef soup, dumplings, and locally made Tolmin cheese rising from the valley all around.

If you're lucky you may even see Goldhorn. Legend has it that these mountains are the home of 'white women', or fairies, that would help travellers in need and tend to their flocks high on the mountain slopes. The leader of their herd was a giant white steinbock, called Goldhorn, whose magic horns, it is said, point the way to a secret treasure, still hidden in the mountains to this day.

True or not, the real treasure is the park itself. Few mountain ranges are more filled with life and culture and the endless creativity of nature, than the Alps. This little corner of that great range may not be the best known, but it may just be the most beautiful of all.

WHERE: North-west Slovenia, 40 miles north of Ljubljana. The nearby towns of Ribčev Laz, Ukanc and Stara Fužina make good bases: *www.tnp.si*

DON'T MISS: Hiking the Soča Trail, which follows the beautiful emerald green Soča River peacefully for fifteen blissful miles, passing through three spectacular gorges along the way.

TOP TIP: Spend at least one night in a high-alpine hut. There are various mountain refuges within the park, all in idyllic settings, but the Vodnik Hut, with views of Mount Triglav in the background, is one of the best. Even better, plan out a multi-day hut-to-hut hike to take in many of the park's most spectacular locations without ever having to leave the high country. Book well in advance:
www.tnp.si/en/visit/in-natures-heart

WHILE YOU'RE THERE: Visit Lake Bled, just five miles to the east of the park, a beautiful fairy tale lake with a tear-shaped island in the middle and warm, thermal-heated waters perfect for a swim. Paddle out to the island, ring the bell of the church there and, legend has it, your wishes will come true: *www.bled.si*

GOREME HISTORICAL NATIONAL PARK, TURKEY

Goreme Historical National Park, in Cappadocia, Turkey is one of the most surreal landscapes on the planet. Millions of years of erosion has carved enormous towers, called 'fairy chimneys' from the surrounding volcanic rocks. Pinnacles rise like castle turrets from the desert, streaked in red and ochre; there are spires, over a hundred feet tall, adorned in rocky crowns and stone totems chiselled from the orange and yellow sediment of ancient volcanic ash. The entire landscape feels sculpted, like a petrified forest, a garden of bizarre statues crafted in wind and rain.

But it's what's inside the towers that's really special. The volcanic tuff of the area is soft and easy to mould. So, starting around 1200 BC, or potentially even earlier, the people here took a cue from nature and began hollowing out vast refuges from inside the rock itself, many of which still stand today. But these aren't ordinary caves. Elaborate homes with doors, windows, staircases and carved facades scatter the hillsides like architectural honeycomb. One of the best examples is the former town of Zelve, in the north of the park, a vast network of intricate cave dwellings, like ancient apartment blocks, hollowed out from the valley as if part of some fairy tale kingdom.

Even more impressive are the underground cities. Cappadocia was in a difficult position. Because of their location on the doorstep of marauding armies of Greeks, Persians and others, as well as their early adoption of Christianity and subsequent threat from Muslim invaders and later the Turks, they needed a defence. But rather than run, the people of Cappadocia chose to dig instead. To date,

Photo: Arian Zwegers

36 underground cities have been excavated, but it is thought many dozens more are waiting to be discovered.

The largest is Derinkuyu. On the surface, there are about 600 outside doors, each one concealed cleverly in courtyards and homes. From there, a network of tunnels and carved staircases descend downwards, connecting family living spaces with communal areas: a labyrinth of homes, cellars, kitchens, stables, churches, even wineries and a school. In total, Derinkuyu extends close to 300 feet from the surface to its lowest level, eighteen floors underground – exactly like a modern skyscraper, but inverted. There are wells, water tanks, niches for oil lamps, and at least 15,000 ventilation shafts that provide fresh air to even the deepest layers. As many as 20,000 people could have resided here comfortably for weeks and months. When danger loomed on the horizon, the villagers simply abandoned their homes on the surface and retreated underground with their livestock, valuables and supplies, sealing the entrance tunnels with large stone doors that could only be operated from the inside. They were clever too, disguising air holes as wells and staggering cooking areas, so the smoke dispersed over a wide area.

Just as beautiful are the rock-cut churches. Dating from around the 10th to the 12th century, these extravagant Byzantine chapels, cathedrals and monastic complexes, hewn directly from the mountains, are decorated inside with colourful frescoes of Biblical scenes, saints and religious iconography. The Goreme Open-Air Museum now contains many of the region's finest examples: eleven principal buildings in all, some multiple stories tall, others carved inside with columns and arches, just as impressive as any European counterpart of the time. The Tokali Church is one of the largest in the area, with its vaulted ceiling painted in rich bands of indigo, red and blue, depicting the life of Christ in exquisite detail; the Elmali Church, four columns and a domed ceiling covered in hues of red ochre that narrate the story of Abraham. Karanlik, the Dark Church, is named for its lack of windows, which has preserved the colours inside the cave as vividly as the day they were first painted.

Elsewhere, there is much else to explore too, with dozens of miles of hiking paths leading between many of the main sites. The supremely bizarre Paşabağ, with its mushroom-like rock spires, surrounded by vineyards of sweet local wine; the formations of the Devrent Valley, like a petrified menagerie: look closely and you'll see camels, snakes, dolphins and even a dragon enshrined in stone. Uchisar Castle is a natural fortress, formed from the tallest fairy chimney in the region, with uninterrupted panoramas of the entire park.

These are the landscapes of dreams, a surreal world painted in the fiery colours of the desert, where cities spiral in labyrinths underground and churches are cut straight from the mountain side. Goreme National Park, and the ancient rock sites of Cappadocia that connect to it are a genuine wonder of the world, a fairy tale kingdom where human culture and ingenuity is intertwined with the breathtaking aesthetics of the land itself.

WHERE: Cappadocia, East-central Anatolia, Turkey. The nearest town is Goreme: *www.goturkeytourism.com/things-to-do/goreme-national-park-rock-sites-cappadocia-unesco-turkey.html*

DON'T MISS: Taking a balloon ride over the national park and surrounding valleys, one of the most spectacular places in the world to do so.

TOP TIP: Stay in a cave hotel to experience the life of Cappadocia's early settlers, though with a lot more comfort

– some of the most beautiful boutique hotels in the country are built within these ancient caverns. The Fairy Chimney Inn is a good option: *www.fairychimney.com*

WHILE YOU'RE THERE: The Aladağlar National Park is only a couple of hours away and filled with some of Turkey's most spectacular mountain scenery – perfect for hiking, climbing and bird watching, with many rare and endemic species: *www.goturkeytourism.com*

VATNAJÖKULL NATIONAL PARK, ICELAND

Iceland is bubbling hot pools, beaches where crystalline icebergs wash ashore and geysers that erupt hundreds of feet into the air. It is volcanoes and glaciers, fireworks of red hot lava and ice caverns of pure cobalt blue. Few places in the world match its diversity and dangerous beauty. The ground vents heat like breath. Eruptions are the norm, not the exception. Tectonic plates collide and rip fissures, like dark scars, across the burning ground. Iceland is a glimpse at the Earth in its infancy, raw and still forming. You can see it unfold before your eyes.

Especially at Vatnajökull National Park. Covering 5,300 square miles of South-east Iceland, 13 per cent of the entire country, this is the largest national park in Europe, and one of the wildest and most diverse too. At its centre is the Vatnajökull glacier itself, an enormous 3,200-square-mile sheet of ice, larger than all of mainland Europe's glaciers combined. Entire mountain ranges and colossal volcanoes – including Iceland's largest and most active – are buried beneath it. Glacier rivers spill down from it, like frozen fingers grasping for the lowlands, depositing vast beaches of black volcanic sand along the rugged coast.

The south of the park, in a region known as Skaftafell, is characterised by high mountain ridges, including Iceland's tallest peak, Hvannadalshnúkur, standing at over 6,000 feet tall. The trekking is superb; the scenery desolate and sublime. At Glacier Lagoon, icebergs calved from the main cap float on the dazzling blue waters of the bay – one of the highlights of the park. At Diamond Beach, they wash up on the dark sand like crystal statues, glistening in the sunlight.

To the north, in Jökulsárgljúfur, the volcano Snaefell – the entry point for Jules Verne's fictional *Journey to the Centre of the Earth* – dominates the skyline, along with the towering mesa Herdubreid, which Icelanders call the Queen of the Mountains, rising more than 5,000 feet from the volcanic plains. Huge canyons, formed by glacier floods thousands of years ago, are carved into the land here – the most stunning of which is Ásbyrgi, a half-mile-long horseshoe-shaped gorge with sheer 330-foot cliffs on all sides, created, legend has it, by the Norse god Odin's eight-legged horse, Sleipnir, as he rode by.

Just as spectacular is Dettifoss – the largest waterfall by volume in Europe, a staggering torrent 330 feet wide and 144 feet tall. But unlike other giant cascades around the world, there are no barriers here, meaning it's possible to walk right up to its rocky edge – like staring over an abyss of mist and thunder, too powerful and deafening to be real. Nearby is the beautiful Lake Askja, Iceland's deepest lake, formed in 1875 after a powerful eruption caused the magma chamber at the heart of the Askja volcano to collapse. But even better are the warm milky waters of Lake Viti next door to it, another crater lake, but this one geothermally heated,

Photo: Adam Jang

creating what is, perhaps, the world's largest hot tub and one of the best soaks you'll ever have.

But the fun doesn't have to stop at the park's boundaries. In the Golden Circle, Iceland's celebrated touring route, there is the dramatic Gullfoss waterfall, the stunningly beautiful geothermic geyser field, the famed Blue Lagoon and more. Just a few miles outside of Reykjavik, the country's idyllic capital city on the coast, there are rivers to raft, extreme 4x4 jeep safaris, dog-sledding, skiing, as well as some of the best snorkelling and scuba diving in the world, including the only place on the planet where you can dive between two tectonic plates. Iceland is adventure and awe, the Earth at its most raw and dynamic, where glaciers and volcanoes battle in endless cycles, here, in the land of fire and ice.

WHERE: South-east Iceland. There are numerous gateway towns for the park, depending on where you want to explore. See website for details: *www.vatnajokulsthjodgardur.is/en*

DON'T MISS: The natural ice caves inside the Vatnajökull glacier itself. Large enough to hike through, these spectacular caverns glow luminous blue inside, a frozen world unlike anywhere else on the planet. Numerous tour operators offer various trips, from easy family-friendly walk-throughs to full on ice-caving expeditions. Glacier Guides is a good option: *www.glacierguides.is*

TOP TIP: Come in summer to experience the midnight sun. Because Iceland is so close to the Arctic Circle, during the months of June and July the sun never sets, meaning your adventures never have to stop either. For the Northern Lights, come in September or October or in February or March for the most spectacular displays.

WHILE YOU'RE THERE: Check out Iceland's other national parks: Snæfellsjökull, along the beautiful coasts of the western peninsula, and the spectacular Thingvellir, home of many of the Golden Circle's highlights as well as the national shrine of Iceland – one of the best places to learn about the country's unique culture and history: *www.iceland.is*

THE NATIONAL PARK, GREENLAND

Greenland's only national park (simply called, The National Park) is the biggest protected nature reserve in the world. Encompassing an astonishing 375,000 square miles of pristine arctic wilderness, it is 28 times larger than America's biggest park, Wrangell–St. Elias in Alaska, and more than 200 times the size of the Cairngorms National Park in the UK. It dwarfs the entire countries of France and Spain, is more than double the size of Germany, and makes Texas look like a little backwater town. If it were a country it would be the 31st largest in the world.

The sense of remoteness is palpable. In this vast swathe of polar ice and high barren tundra there are fewer than 50 permanent residents. Most of those are researchers, seasonal hunters and work crews. Only 500 tourists a year set foot here. It is one of the last untouched tracts of true wilderness on the planet, a place to connect with nature on her terms, where the adventures are as bold and big as the land itself.

Much of the park is covered in ice, in places reaching close to 10,000 feet thick. In fact, Greenland itself, located just 460 miles from the North Pole, is home to the largest ice cap in the world outside of Antarctica – more than 80 per cent of the country is covered by it. But that doesn't mean the park is all desolate and white. There are towering mountains, many never climbed before, windswept high arctic plains, forests that turn golden in autumn and arctic blueberries that colour the spring.

Perhaps most spectacular of all though is Scoresby Sund, on the south-east edge of the park. At approximately 70 miles long, with dozens of side fjords stretching over 100 miles further inland from there, this is the world's largest fjord system, covering an area of roughly 14,700 square miles, and arguably the most beautiful too: a maze of inlets and coves with sheer basalt walls 5,000 feet tall, and luminous blue icebergs, like crystal skyscrapers, floating in the bay.

The wildlife is superb too. Forty per cent of the world's musk oxen reside here along with walruses, caribou, arctic wolves, reindeer and the mighty polar bear. Humpback whales, orcas and seals hug the coast. Halibut, flounder and salmon teem in the icy waters; seabirds, and the majestic white-tailed eagle, fill the sky.

Adventure is everywhere. There are wild hikes where almost no one has trod before, camping out overnight in remote mountain huts, glaciers to scale, snow-fields and unmarked peaks to ski. Join local hunters on dog-sleds searching for musk-oxen; sail out with local fishermen, learning to catch the traditional way; and above it all, for much of the year, there are some of the brightest displays of the Aurora Borealis in the world.

Even better is the chance to share in Greenland's proud indigenous culture first hand. Approximately 90 per cent of the country is Inuit. The first people, it is believed, arrived here close to 5,000 years ago, using the islands of the Canadian Arctic as stepping stones on a long migration from North America. Today's population is descended from a group known as the Thule, who spread across the coasts in the 10th century. Proficient whale and seal hunters, they built the first kayaks (the national symbol of Greenland today), harpoons and dog sleds and their way of life is still embraced. The people live off the land; they build their own boats, carve traditional soapstone figurines and perform drum dances, passing myths and stories down through the generations. The philosophy of their ancestors was to live at one with nature, and that is still how they live to this day: following the seasons, taking only what they need to survive.

It's a good metaphor for the national park itself. Greenland is a place of extremes: superlative scenery, true wilderness, the chance to experience an ancient and still thriving arctic culture. But more than that it's a place to feel humbled by the sheer size and pristine emptiness of nature herself, the roll of the seasons, the call of her untrammelled trails.

WHERE: North-east Greenland. The nearest town is Ittoqqortoormiit: *www.visitgreenland.com*

DON'T MISS: Kayaking along the coast, a fantastic way to get up close to a wide range of marine life and connect with a traditional Inuit way of life.

TOP TIP: If you can afford it, an expedition cruise is an excellent way to see the national park. Numerous operators depart from Reykjavik, Iceland and Spitsbergen, Norway. If travelling independently, you will need to buy a permit before entering the park. Base yourself in the nearby town of Ittoqqortoormiit and hire local guides from there. Come summer for the midnight sun, hiking and kayaking and winter for dog sledding and the Northern Lights.

Photo: Jerzy Strzelecki

Hurtigruten (*www.hurtigruten.com*) and Quark Expeditions (*www.quarkexpeditions.com*) are two good options.

WHILE YOU'RE THERE: Explore some of Greenland's other highlights, including the Ilulissat Icefjord, where about 20 billion tons of icebergs calve into the fjord every year; the trekking around colourful Disko Bay, where the mountains meet the fjords, and the museums and cultural centres of capital city Nuuk.

AFRICA

SERENGETI NATIONAL PARK, TANZANIA

The vast plains of the Serengeti, which encompass the Serengeti National Park in Tanzania, as well as the Maasai Mara Game Reserve across the border in Kenya, are the home of the greatest collection of wildlife on Earth. Although two separate reserves (of which the Serengeti, in Tanzania, is the only official national park), they are one ecosystem, intact, with no barriers bar the ones we draw in our minds.

When British hunter-turned-conservationist Stewart Edward White first set foot here in 1913, providing one of the first detailed accounts of the area, he described it as 'paradise'. The Maasai, who have grazed their cattle here for centuries, and continue to do so today, have another word for it: *siringitu*, from which the name Serengeti is derived: 'the place where the land moves on forever'. It is a fitting description. Not just because of its size: 12,000 square miles of wide-open grasslands that disappear to a seemingly infinite green horizon, like an ocean swaying in the breeze, but because life is in constant movement, like a dance, life and death, circular, unending. The Serengeti is the heartbeat of Africa itself.

The wildlife within the Serengeti National Park itself is, of course, spectacular. Hippos splash in waterholes, elephants march across the savannah, clearing all in their path. In a single glance, it's possible to see zebras, hyenas, giraffes, cheetah, leopards and, king of them all, the mighty lion – more than 2,000 in all, the largest population in Africa by some counts – their roar like a storm that bristles the neck of even the most seasoned of travellers.

Over the border, in Kenya's Maasai Mara Game Reserve, Africa's top safari destination, the game-viewing is perhaps even more concentrated. Where Serengeti National Park follows seasonal patterns, Maasai Mara offers more year-round opportunities and a landscape that is more varied, filled with acacia trees and the mighty Mara River, where Nile crocodiles, 14 feet long, lurk in the murky waters, waiting for prey.

But, undoubtedly, the absolute highlight of any trip to the Serengeti is the Great Migration. This annual 1,000-mile journey of over 1 million wildebeest, as well as hundreds of thousands of ungulates, is the largest land migration in the animal kingdom. Herds stretch 25 miles long, filling the horizon with a storm of dusty mist; the ground shakes for miles around; the noise is like thunder. To see the Great Migration first hand is, perhaps, the most spectacular wildlife show on Earth.

But it's also one of the world's hardest journeys. Predators stalk the herds throughout; river crossings are filled with peril; drought and starvation are a constant threat. In a

Photo: Michelle Maria

single year, 250,000 wildebeest will die, but their movement is the lifeblood of the plains: cropping grass, fertilizing the soil and providing vital nourishment for predators. Without the Great Migration, that constant movement, that dance, the Serengeti would simply cease to exist.

It is a true wonder of the natural world, but it's not the only one here. The Ngorongoro Crater Conservation Area, a 3,200-square-mile reserve which is connected directly to the south-east corner of the Serengeti National Park, protects one of the most beautiful landscapes in all of Africa: a giant caldera, the largest unflooded volcanic crater on Earth, with sheer walls that rise nearly 2,000 feet around it and all the large land animals of Africa within. If there is a paradise on Earth then this is about as close as it comes.

Which makes sense, because this may be first home. Inside this incredible reserve is the Olduvai Gorge, where some of our oldest human ancestors have been found. It is known as the cradle of mankind, the place where we first left the safety of the forest and walked upright into the savannah, beginning a journey of exploration and discovery that continues to this day.

That's what makes the Serengeti so powerful. When we come here, we return to the source. The biologist George Schaller said: 'No one can return from the Serengeti unchanged.' It becomes a part of you; but then again, perhaps it always has been.

WHERE: Northern Tanzania. There are three main gates into the park. The most popular is the Naabi Hill gate, 150 miles west of the nearest main city, Arusha, from where there are connecting small-plane flights directly into the interior of the park: *www.serengeti.org*

DON'T MISS: The chance to meet and talk with local Maasai tribesmen and women. Look for sustainable tour operators that work directly with local tribes in order to make sure your visit benefits them directly. Even better, spend a night in a Maasai village, learning about their culture and partaking in the daily life of the tribe. *www.responsibletravel.com* has some well-vetted options for both.

TOP TIP: Time your visit with the migration cycles of the wildebeest, but cross your fingers too: the exact dates of the migration are dependent on rain and vary each year. July–October is generally the best time to go to the Maasai Mara Game Reserve, in Kenya. January–March is calving season around the Ngorongoro Crater, in Tanzania, while April–June the herds travel through central and western parts of the Serengeti National Park.

WHILE YOU'RE THERE: The Ngorongoro Crater Conservation area, also in Tanzania, is a must. Maasai Mara Game Reserve, in Kenya, is another good option for a Serengeti safari and could be paired with a trip here or done as an alternative. But consider timing your visit with a stop to Lake Natron, less than 100 miles east of Serengeti National Park, too. Each year, over 1 million pink flamingos, some 75 per cent of the world's population, descend on the lake to lay their eggs and raise their chicks. Sir David Attenborough called it: 'one of the world's greatest wildlife attractions', and it is easily combined with any trip to Serengeti National Park. Peak activity is usually between October and early December: *www.tanzaniatourism.go.tz*
www.ngorongorocrater.org
www.magicalkenya.com

VOLCANOES NATIONAL PARK, RWANDA

The Virunga Mountains, of Rwanda, Uganda and the Democratic Republic of Congo, are the best place in the world to see mountain gorillas in the wild. These enormous primates, whose population numbers fewer than 1,000, are one of the world's most amazing animals. Highly intelligent – in captivity they have been able to learn sign language to the level of a three-year-old child – with strong familial bonds and playful, toddler-like young, they are more like us, than not. To see one up close is to understand immediately our existential bond. Look in their eyes and you will see yourself reflected back.

There are three contiguous national parks in the Virunga range and it's possible to see mountain gorillas in each one. But Volcanoes National Park, in Rwanda, is special. Not only is the infrastructure more developed, meaning it's quicker to reach the park (roughly two hours from the airport) and often easier to see the gorillas when you get there, its award-winning conservation model is also largely responsible for a surprising resurgence in gorilla numbers in the area.

In the mid-1980s the number of mountain gorillas left in the wild had dropped to just 300, near extinction level, as a result of poaching and deforestation. Volcanoes National Park changed all that. Their model gives 20 per cent of the park's revenue back to the communities that surround it, helping to fund schools, health centres and conservation programmes as well as set up income-generating projects that tap into the local tourism economy. Ensuring that these communities benefit from the park has drastically reduced the level of poaching (which is more often than not accidental: gorillas become snared in traps intended for buffalo or antelope). In a world of despairing wildlife news, Volcanoes National Park is a rare beacon of hope. When you come here, you not only see one of the world's most extraordinary animals, you help save them too; and it's all thanks to one remarkable woman.

Dian Fossey, the famed American primatologist (whose life the film *Gorillas in the Mist* was based upon) came here in 1967 and set up camp on the slopes of Mount Karisimbi: two makeshift tents, that she called Karisoke, and that would become one of the most celebrated research stations in the world. She would spend the next twelve years living with the gorillas, imitating their behaviour to gain acceptance: 'knuckle-walking' on all fours or chewing stalks of celery to play on their natural curiosity, while at the same time publicising to the wider world the true gentle nature, and surprising intelligence, of these once-feared distant cousins.

But she wasn't just a passive observer. Appalled by the killing of innocent gorillas, she soon took matters into her own hands, taking on the poachers and cattle herders directly with increasingly severe tactics: burning snares, spray-painting herds, self-funding anti-poaching units, raising awareness around the world, even wearing masks to scare them away. That mountain gorilla numbers are climbing today and not on the long list of animals lost forever is because of her.

But it came at a price: on 27 December 1985, Dian Fossey was found brutally murdered in the cabin of her research station. There was evidence of forced entry but no signs that robbery had been committed; the killer has still never been caught.

Today, there are two primary troops of mountain gorillas in Volcanoes National Park: the Sabyinyo group, which is

Photo: Neil Palmer (CIAT)

smaller and more accessible, usually located closer to the park's boundaries, and the Titus group, ancestors of the original troop studied by Fossey, usually found deeper in the forest. In most cases, the trek to reach either group is hard: sometimes taking many hours bushwhacking through thick bamboo and unmarked jungle trails, steep, muddy and overgrown. But the hour you spend with the gorillas, who now view their human admirers as more of a curiosity than a threat, is worth the effort. Less than 30 feet away, you can see a family of dozens, mothers with six-month-old infants suckling on their breasts, toddlers wrestling in trees, the mighty silverback – three times the size of an average man – keeping watch, beating his chest, charging through the undergrowth in terrifying displays of his strength and dominance. There is, perhaps, no other wildlife experience on the planet more exhilarating, where animals of such power allow such close proximity and whose strength is matched only by their gentleness and the bonds of friendship and family we so recognise in ourselves.

Just as remarkable as the resurgence of mountain gorillas in Rwanda is the resurgence of the country itself. Devastated by years of civil unrest and, in 1994, one of the worst genocides in human history, in which close to 1 million ethnic Tutsis were brutally murdered by their fellow countrymen, Rwanda has now transformed itself into one of Africa's safest and most progressive nations. The fight to protect the mountain gorillas, those remarkable distant cousins of ours, is far from over; there is much work still to be done. But here, in Volcanoes National Park, the best place in the world to see these remarkable animals up close, they are making a comeback – just like the country itself; and you can be part of that comeback too. Dian would have been proud.

WHERE: Northern Rwanda. The nearest town, and main hub for gorilla tracking expeditions, is Ruhengeri: *www.volcanoesnationalparkrwanda.com*

DON'T MISS: Aside from the gorilla trekking, which is obviously the main draw, make sure to take a tour of the Iby'Iwacu cultural village for a unique insight into Rwandan culture, with the chance to take part in traditional arts and crafts, archery, cultural performances and more.

TOP TIP: Time your visit with the annual Kwita Izina, or gorilla naming ceremony, which takes place each September – a huge celebration that is a key part of the park's conservation strategy and success. Visit the Dian Fossey Foundation's website for more information on gorilla conservation in Rwanda: *www.gorillafund.org*

WHILE YOU'RE THERE: Spend a day at the nearby Gishwati-Mukuru National Park, less than an hour away. This beautiful forest is home to five primate species, including a troop of chimpanzees – a rare chance to see these intelligent, social creatures up close in the wild: *www.rwandatourism.com*

NORTH LUANGWA NATIONAL PARK, ZAMBIA

North Luangwa National Park, in Zambia, is unlike any other national park in Africa. There are no roads, no cars, no permanent lodges, and no way to enter, save through a handful of carefully selected operators. Only 500 people a year visit. This is the real Africa, not a show for tourists. You

Photo: Paul Maritz

come for the solitude, the empty space, for the world without geometric lines. You come to commune with nature, to feel the wilderness pressing around you, the danger, the silence, the Earth for your bed, the stars for your blanket. You come to experience the Africa of old.

But there's only one way you can. The walking safari was pioneered here, in North Luangwa's more popular sister park, South Luangwa, in the 1950s, and here it still reigns. The concept, first adapted from anti-poaching patrols, is simple: low impact, sustainable wildlife experiences that offer a more serene, intimate connection to the land, one that is reminiscent of the experience of early explorers and the indigenous people; the Ngoni and others that have made their home here for millennia. If you want to see North Luangwa National Park there's only one way you can: on your own two feet.

That's a big deal. Sure, you may cover more ground and, likely, see more animals in a car, but the car is a safety net between you and the wild. On your feet, you are not the fastest, nor the strongest, animal out there. Led by an expert guide, who carries a rifle (though, usually, just for warning shots), you are relatively safe. But relative is one thing at home and another staring down a pride of lions, blood from a fresh kill dripping down their mane; or facing a matriarch elephant as she mock charges, trunk and ears flaring in aggression; or crouching in the undergrowth as a herd of buffalo kick up a dust storm around you as they gallop past. Walking safaris are thrilling, dangerous, humbling things.

But they are also peaceful and even enlightening. Inside the park the only accommodation is in remote camps, which are erected and then dismantled at the start and end of every season. Each one is different, but all are constructed from natural, local materials and placed in exquisite wildlife-rich locations. Mwaleshi Camp, four chalets nestled among a grove of mopane trees on a scenic bend of the Mwaleshi River, not far from a pod of 400 hippos. Buffalo Camp, seven thatched cabins and a delightful bar/ restaurant frequented by elephants, buffalo and the cackle of hyenas echoing through the dark. Each day begins at dawn, listening to the sounds of the awakening wilderness, and ends by the fireside, sharing stories, or gazing at the impossibly bright canopy of African stars. North Luangwa is about the thrill of the wild, but it's about intimacy too, a gradual enrichment, rather than lists of animals to tick.

But that's not to say the wildlife is sparse. The park is noted for its massive herds of buffalo and large prides of lion – it's not uncommon to see the two locked in a struggle for life and death – as well as the highest density of hippos in the world. There are wildebeest, zebra, baboons, vervet monkeys and a host of birds, including giant eagle owls and more. But the most special animal here is the black rhino. Forty years ago Zambia had Africa's largest population of black rhinos, 12,000 in all with 4,000 here in the Luangwa Valley. Twenty years later they were all gone, wiped out by illegal poaching. But now they're back. In 2003, five black rhinos were reintroduced to the park, flown in and then gradually released into the wild. Ten more came in 2006, then five more in 2008. Today, there are more than 30 free roaming black rhinoceros in the park, all fiercely guarded by North Luangwa's strict anti-poaching programmes – one of the most positive African conservation stories of recent years.

But, in the end, North Luangwa isn't about what you see, but how you see it. It's about the silence, the stars, the sounds of the savannah filtering through the canvas at dawn; it's about meeting the wilderness on equal terms; that thrill, that danger, but the serenity and humility too. It's about finding the real Africa, outside and inside of you. And there's only one way to do it: on your own two feet.

WHERE: Northern Zambia. The nearest town is Mwaleshi: *www.zambiatourism.com/destinations/national-parks/north-luangwa-national-park*

DON'T MISS: If you can afford it, camping out in one of the park's remote fly-in bush camps is a once-in-a-lifetime experience not to be missed. Only two operators are allowed to run them; both are excellent: Remote African Safaris (*www.remoteafrica.com*) and Shiwa Safaris (*www.shiwasafaris.com*).

TOP TIP: The remote bush camps can be expensive, for a more cost-effective option try Camp Zambia. These basic campsites offer places to pitch a tent and simple cooking and washing facilities. Although less remote, they are set in beautiful, wild locations and offer a unique African camping experience: *www.campzambia.com*

WHILE YOU'RE THERE: Visit North Luangwa's sister park, South Luangwa National Park, just a few miles to the south and easily combined in a single trip. Offering more traditional safaris, as well as walking ones, the experience is less exclusive but often more affordable and just as wildlife-rich: *www.zambiatourism.com*

CHOBE NATIONAL PARK, BOTSWANA

Chobe National Park, in Northern Botswana, is the best place in the world to see elephants in the wild. Together with its neighbour, the spectacular Okavango Delta, one of the most important ecosystems on the planet, these 4,500 square miles of the Great Rift Valley are home to roughly 120,000 elephants, the highest concentration on Earth. Come in the dry season, between April and October, and you'll find dozens of families bathing in waterholes, herds a thousand strong marching across the floodplains, surrounding you, trumpeting warnings, shaking the ground beneath your feet.

They are one of the world's most remarkable animals. Highly intelligent, recent scientific studies have shown that they are able to use tools, differentiate between human languages (those of the Maasai men who hunt them, for example, elicit different reactions from those of other tribes, who do not) and adapt their behaviour to defend against poachers (for example, using watering holes in dangerous areas only at night when the risk of human contact is less). Perhaps most famously, they are able to remember complex cognitive maps of spatial environments, helping them to migrate between seasonal watering holes often over vast distances.

But just as startling as their brains is the richness of their emotional lives: parents comfort their young in a way that is usually only seen in other primates; they are playful, social and incredibly self-aware – able to recognise themselves in a mirror – one of the very few animals on Earth, other than humans, that can do so. Most astonishing of all, they mourn their dead. Elephants will defend the body of a family

Photo: Gorgo

member or friend and they seem curious, even sad, about the bones of their fallen, often stopping to investigate them – a behaviour we don't yet fully understand.

All of which makes their slaughter infinitely more harrowing. It is estimated that 100 elephants are killed in Africa every single day for their ivory tusks, a product which has been scientifically proven to have no medicinal value despite its high demand in Chinese and other markets. As a result, their numbers are plummeting. In the early 20th century, millions of elephants roamed this continent, from the plains of Cape Town to the slopes of Mount Kilimanjaro; now only 400,000 remain. Chobe is one of their last strongholds.

The park is composed of four main ecosystems. The first is the Chobe River itself, one of Africa's most beautiful and life-sustaining rivers, a silver ribbon flowing through the stark sands of the Kalahari Desert that teems with thousands of buffalo, waterbuck, impala, puku, hippos and crocodiles. Vast numbers of elephants come here to wait out the long drought of summer. Forty miles to the south are the Ngwenzumba Pans, colossal clay pans that fill with water in the rainy season, drawing enormous herds. To the west is the remote Savuté Marsh, a 60-mile channel of the Linyanti River (itself, another key habitat of the park), where prides of lion, hyenas and leopards stalk their prey through the long swampy grass. Giraffes and zebra roam free; baboons and monkeys fill the trees. Chobe National Park is a paradise of big game where the dramas of life and death, drought and abundance, play out in endless cycles, like night fading to day.

But what makes it one of the greatest parks in the world is not just what's happening inside its boundaries, but what's available on its doorstep too. Just a couple of hours away, on the Zambia–Zimbabwe border, is Victoria Falls, the largest single drop waterfall on the planet – over a mile wide and 360 feet tall at its peak. To the local Kololo tribe, it is known as Mosi-oa-Tunya, The Smoke that Thunders: 1 million litres of raging torrent pouring over its lip every second, spray shooting 1,000 feet in the air, sparkling with rainbows in a mist that can be seen from twenty miles away.

Yet, perhaps even more impressive, in its own way, is the Okavango Delta, a short one-hour flight south. This vital wetland, the world's only inland delta, is formed as the Okavango River discharges into the Kalahari Desert, creating a huge oasis that supports one of the greatest concentrations of wildlife on the continent. In the dry season, animals congregate here in staggering numbers, including some of the world's most critically endangered species: white and black rhinoceros, African wild dogs, cheetahs, lions and more. Watching the transformation during the rainy season of dry, barren desert into an almost impossibly verdant and thriving wetland, filled with palm-fringed islands and waterways, is nothing short of miraculous.

That's why Chobe is so unique. Not only is it one of the last bastions of hope for the African elephant, a wild sanctuary where tens of thousands gather on the banks of that great river; nor is it just one of Africa's most abundant wildlife parks, where the cyclical dramas of life and death unfold before your very eyes. It's also perfectly placed for one of the most diverse African adventures on the planet (matched only by the Serengeti): the desert, the delta, wildlife, a wonder of the world, all in one breathtaking single trip.

WHERE: Northern Botswana. The nearest town, and gateway to the park, is Kasane: *www.chobenationalpark.com*

DON'T MISS: Taking a houseboat down the Chobe River.

These live-aboard boutique small ship cruises are the perfect way to experience life in the park: sunrise breakfast on the deck; sundowners, stars and the sounds of Africa each evening: *www.chobenationalpark.co.za/chobe-houseboats*

TOP TIP: Come to Chobe in the dry season, May to September, when animals congregate around the river, for the best wildlife experience. The Okavango Delta is best seen when it is flooded, from June to October. Victoria Falls are at their most impressive during their high-water period, February to June. If you want to see all three at the perfect time, June is the month to do it.

WHILE YOU'RE THERE: Victoria Falls and the Okavango Delta are a must (for the latter, the Moremi Game Reserve offers one of the best experiences) and can easily be combined in a single trip. But, if you have time, consider visiting the Central Kalahari Game Reserve as well, one of Africa's largest and most adventurous wilderness reserves filled with sand dunes, forests of acacia trees and the ancestral lands of the San Bushmen: *www.botswanatourism.co.bw*

NAMIB-SKELETON COAST NATIONAL PARK, NAMIBIA

The Namib-Skeleton Coast National Park, in Namibia, is the largest national park in Africa. Stretching 976 miles along the entire length of Namibia's coast, it covers a total area of 41,562 square miles – larger than Switzerland, Belgium and the Netherlands combined.

At its heart is the Namib Desert. Covering the entire western expanse of the country, it is thought to be the most ancient desert on Earth, some 43 million years old, shifting windswept dunes that roll on endlessly to the sea. But the park itself is relatively new. Established in 2011, it is a consolidation of three pre-existing protected reserves: Sperrgebiet, in the south, Namib-Naukluft, in the centre, and the infamous Skeleton Coast, in the north.

The central portion is, perhaps, the most spectacular. Here, in the Naukluft Mountains, on the eastern edge of the park – one of the few reliable sources of water in the area – the hiking is superb: hard ochre ridges that rise from the shimmering plains of the desert, filled with rare mountain zebra, black-backed jackal, leopards, wild cats and hundreds of species of birds, lizards and nocturnal beasts that somehow manage to eke out life from the hot stones.

Further north, at Brandberg Mountain, known as the 'fire mountain' because of the way the setting sun causes the dark granite to glow like the embers of giant flame, is one of the richest collections of rock art in the world, more than 43,000 documented paintings in some 879 individual sites. Drawn between 2,000 and 4,000 years ago by the ancestors of today's San Bushmen, using animal bones, charcoal, blood and plants collected nearby, the images are a startlingly detailed depiction of their everyday life: human figures adorned in headdresses; a giraffe standing in a shower of rain; two naked men hunting a springbok, firing arrows as it leaps away.

But it's the dunes at Sossusvlei that truly take your breath away. These colossal red mountains of sand are among the largest dunes on the planet, some, like the aptly named 'Big Daddy', reach higher than 1,000 feet – taller than the tip of The Shard, in London. Climb to the top, especially at dawn and

Photo: Laika ac

dusk when the colours are strongest and the low sun shadows the dune field in perfect symmetry, and it's like being on another planet: dark wind-scoured trees silhouetted against the primary red of the desert like a modern art collage. If you want to experience the silence and unfathomable emptiness of the desert, to hear the sands sing on the wind, the hot breeze, the colours evolving with the day, shadows playing on the horizon like vast sculptures of the Earth, then it is to here, Sossusvlei, that you must come.

The far north is made up of the Skeleton Coast. The Bushmen call it 'The Land God Made in Anger', the Portuguese called it 'The Gates of Hell'; we know it as one of the most desolate and dangerous landscapes on Earth. Dense fog and violent surf have created the largest shipwreck gravesite in the world here – 6,000 square miles of sand dunes, arid mountains and the rusting frames of withered boats buried within, some close to 500 years old. Alongside the skeletons of old whales, beached from violent storms, the bones of sailors can sometimes be found too, bent double, frozen in the sand, crouching for shelter that will never come.

But there's life too. Here in the far north of the park, what looks like wasteland is in fact the ancestral home of the Himba people, some of Namibia's last nomadic pastoralists. Like the desert around them, they are an exquisitely beautiful people, and a good metaphor for why coming here is such a profound experience. Antoine de Saint-Exupéry, the author of *The Little Prince*, wrote that: 'What makes a desert beautiful … is that somewhere it hides a well.' This is the Earth at its most savage. Yet even here, there is colour. Even in the most barren silence and desolate emptiness, life springs forward, painting pictures in the windswept patterns of the sand.

WHERE: The west coast of Namibia. The town of Sesriem, 200 miles south of capital Windhoek, is the main entry point for the Namib-Naukluft portion of the park, with easy access to the Sossusvlei dunes: *www.namibiatourism.com.na*

DON'T MISS: Taking a dawn balloon flight over the Sossusvlei dunes, an incredible way to see this awe-inspiring wonder of the world.

TOP TIP: Safe, friendly and with good roads, Namibia is an ideal place for a self-drive safari. Numerous operators offer self-drive packages, in which they supply the 4x4 vehicle, all the necessary kit and emergency precautions, leaving you to drive out into the wilds of Africa alone – a true adventure that's hard to beat. Safari Drive is a good option: *www.safaridrive.com*

WHILE YOU'RE THERE: Make sure to visit Etosha National Park, in the north of Namibia, just east of the Skeleton Coast. This vast expanse of land, home to rare black rhinos, cheetahs, leopards, elephants, zebras and lions is one of Africa's greatest parks and a near-miss for this book: *www.etoshanationalpark.org*

LA RÉUNION NATIONAL PARK, RÉUNION ISLAND

There is an island in the middle of the Indian Ocean that almost no one knows exists. Owned by France and cousin to its more famous neighbours, Mauritius, 100 miles to the east, and the British Seychelles, to the north, this tiny speck of land, just 39 miles long and 28 miles wide – less than a quarter of the size of Hawaiʻi's Big Island, is nonetheless one of the most remarkable places on Earth. Tropical volcanoes, covered in lush jungle, rise straight from the ocean, 10,000 feet tall: jagged green peaks, with waterfalls tumbling in great thunderous arcs, like a fairy tale picture of paradise. Rainforests teem with dozens of rare endemic birds. There are coral reefs ablaze with rainbows and white-sand beaches lapped by shallow turquoise bays. If there ever was a lost Eden, a place of unimaginable natural beauty, untouched, unknown and hidden from the world, then Réunion Island is surely it.

Unknown, that is, to all but the French, who claimed the island in the 1600s and have been keeping it to themselves since then. But this isn't your average tropical paradise. Sure, there are golden beaches to laze on, a smattering of resorts along the coast; there's snorkelling, surfing and, in the deeper waters outside the reef, dolphins (a new species, the Risso's, was discovered here in 2003) and humpback whales. This being officially a part of France, you won't starve either. But where the island really comes alive is in the interior, in Les Hauts, the high country of La Réunion National Park.

Covering roughly 400 square miles, more than 40 per cent of the island, from basilica-like spires and vast lava plains to deep gorges, rainforests, cloud forests, savannah and tropical lagoons, hiking through La Réunion is like seeing the world in microcosm – much of it absolutely untouched since before the first settlers arrived. At its core are two enormous volcanic massifs. On the eastern end of the island is the 'Piton de la Fournaise', an enormous shield volcano that rises more than 8,000 feet above sea-level and is one of the most active volcanoes in the world. The hike to the top, from the coast and across the lunar landscape of the 'Plaine des Sables' lava field, is one of the best on the island.

To the west is 'Piton des Neiges', Réunion's highest point at just over 10,000 feet, surrounded by three enormous *cirques*; huge, steep-sided, natural amphitheatres, which form the most spectacular area of the park. The Cirque de Mafate is the wildest and most remote, accessible only by foot or helicopter, a vast expanse of Jurassic-like peaks and razor-edge ridges disappearing as far as the eye can see. Settled by runaway slaves in the 19th century, a handful of tiny Creole villages, known as islets, dot the verdant slopes with farms of banana, peach and sugar cane.

To the west, Cirque de Salazie is dominated by the Voile de la Mariée, one of the most beautiful waterfalls on the island: cool white water pouring into a deep blue lagoon, lavish jungle and the soft trickle of dozens of other cascades falling around it on all sides. In its centre, is the delightful hamlet of Hell-Bourg, officially classified as one of France's most beautiful villages: terracotta roofs and white washed stone, balconies and fountains, clouds and mountains far below.

In the south the Cirque de Cilaos, the most populated of the trio, is found at the end of a precipitous mountain road, encircled by sheer cliffs like a secret village lost in time. Its name comes from the local Malagasy word, *tsilaosa*, meaning 'country you don't leave' and it's easy to see why: set on the shores of a beautiful lake, with natural hot springs, fields of wildflowers, waterfalls and (this being France) vineyards producing world-class wine surround it.

But there's another reason why this is Eden too: the people. Réunion Island is a melting pot of culture, with African, Indian, Chinese and French influences among others. But here there's no difference; they're all Creole and proud of it. The descendants of slaves and European settlers live side by side. On one corner, choral music drifts from a Roman Catholic Church, on another the melodic chanting

Photo: Jean-Louis Sicot

of Koranic verse comes through the arched windows of a mosque. A Tamil Temple sits next to a Chinese Pagoda. But they all get along. Diversity is celebrated. That means something. Almost no one knows about this remarkable little island, but perhaps they should. Because a true Eden is not just in the splendour of the natural world around us, but in how we treat each other too. Here, on Réunion Island, they got both right.

WHERE: Réunion Island, Indian Ocean. There are various gateway towns and villages in and around the national park. See website for details: *https://en.reunion.fr*

DON'T MISS: Watching the sunrise from the top of Piton des Neiges. There is a simple mountain hut, *Le refuge de la* Caverne Dufour, just over an hour's hike from the summit, with sleeping space for 48 in basic dormitories. Wake up in the dark, at least two hours before dawn, and you'll be watching the sun rise from the roof of the Indian Ocean. Advance reservations are essential: *www.reunion.fr/planifier/ ou-dormir/gites-d-etapes-ou-de-montagne/refuge-de-la-caverne- dufour-piton-des-neiges-558654*

TOP TIP: Time your visit with the Festival Liberté Métisse, held around 20 December each year, an island-wide celebration in honour of the abolition of slavery. Expect street-parties, Maloya music and dancing with your toes in the sand.

WHILE YOU'RE THERE: Combine a trip to Réunion Island with a safari in Madagascar, just a short plane ride to the east. This incredibly diverse African island has many great national parks, but Ranomafana is one of the best: home to

twelve species of the famous Madagascan lemurs:
www.madagascar-tourisme.com/en

SIMIEN MOUNTAINS NATIONAL PARK, ETHIOPIA

Just north of Ethiopia's Great Rift Valley, surrounded on all sides by the marvels of that great country, is one of the most spectacular landscapes on Earth. The world soars here: grand pinnacles of jungle and stone, sheer ravines, cliffs 3,000 feet deep. Twenty five million years ago, the entire area was covered in thick flows of basalt lava and then whipped clean by colossal storms and glacial scours. The result is fantastic, almost otherworldly: a vast cauldron of axe-wedge gorges and snaking ridges as sharp as a razor's edge. In its centre is the imposing massif of Ras Dashen, one of Africa's tallest peaks, jutting 15,000 feet into the foreboding sky. The ancient Greek poet Homer described the Simien Mountains as 'chess pieces of the gods'. We have another nickname for it: the Grand Canyon of Africa.

But it's not just about the views. The park also protects three key species, which are endemic to the Ethiopian highlands. The king is the Ethiopian wolf, the rarest canid in the world, and Africa's most threatened carnivore with a total population of fewer than 500. Distant relatives of grey wolves, these highly endangered animals, with sharp snouts and distinctive red coats, live on just seven isolated mountain enclaves in the region.

But the king can be hard to see. Much more common is the Walia ibex, which exists here and is endemic to this area alone. Found on steep slopes and rocky crags up to 13,000

Photo: Bernard Gagnon

feet high, the Walia are known for their spectacular ridged horns, which arch back across their body like a long mane that can reach five feet in length. Legend has it, they were brought here by Saint Kidus Yared, the 6th-century Ethiopian musician who is credited with inventing the sacred music of the country, and who used the Walia to carry his holy books.

Even more common (you will practically be falling over them), and the most fun of all, are the gelada monkeys, also known as 'bleeding heart baboons' because of the red mark on their chest. These fascinating animals, that live only in the high mountains of Ethiopia – an environment utterly unlike that occupied by any of their primate cousins – are the world's most terrestrial primate (aside from humans), spending their time on the ground, rather than in trees, grazing fresh grass and foraging for herbs, roots and seeds. They are the last surviving species of a huge range of land-based primates that once spread across this land. Usually living in smaller family units, at times they join together to form enormous bands, more than 1,000 strong, the largest groups of any monkey in the world. But they have an unusual habit. To guard against predation at night, the geladas, who are highly skilled rock climbers, scale down from the top of sheer cliffs to sleep huddled together on narrow ledges, nothing but thousands of feet of air around them on all sides. Watching hundreds of geladas leap from the precipice each sunset, tumbling down the sheer cliffs only to catch themselves at the last minute on tiny holds and tufts of grass, is one of the highlights of the whole park.

Most people come for the trekking though, with the most popular routes weaving between traditional villages, offering a chance to explore the fascinating culture of the Simien people alongside its breathtaking landscapes. In the lower foothills, much of the land is farmed, terraced hillsides ploughed by oxen, with donkeys, goats and barefoot children running around. For thousands of years, these mountains were used as an important trade route and to this day they are surrounded by cultural and historical sites on all sides. Walk these paths and you follow in those footsteps, hiking between simple camps, or homestays in local villages, bedding down in traditional *tukuls* each night: round stone and timber framed homes, with conical thatched roofs, held together by a mixture of mud and cow dung.

To hike the full 111-square-mile park takes about twelve days, covering all the highland must-sees before trekking off the beaten track to the cultivated lowlands, for a deep immersion in the rural life of the Simiens. The most popular route, however, is just four days long and covers much of the park's best scenery and wildlife, walking from the main hub of Debark to the campsites of Sankaber, Geech and Chennek. Each camp has their own affiliated community-run lodge, serving up freshly-cooked Ethiopian delicacies every night, nothing but perfect stars and the howl of wolf packs all around. Highlights along the way include the roughly 2,000-foot-tall stunning Jinbar Waterfall and the 360-degree views from Imet Gogo, a rocky promontory that pokes out 13,000 feet above the park's most stunning viewpoint, earning it the reputation as Africa's Grand Canyon.

But even that comparison falls short. The Simien Mountains are unique, a land infused with ancient culture and rare endemic species, where the furnace of the Earth has carved in lava, glaciers and storm a landscape of dreams. Poetry cannot do it justice: you have to feel it, this playground of the gods, this land of wolves and wild monkeys that leap from the precipice each night.

WHERE: Northern Ethiopia. The nearest town is Debark.

Fly to Gondar, 65 miles to the west: *www.simienmountains.org*

DON'T MISS: Eating traditional Ethiopian food, one of the greatest cuisines in Africa: colourful dishes of stews, salads and spicy beef, scooped up by hand in freshly baked *injera* sourdough bread.

TOP TIP: Make sure to spend a night or two at the park's twelve-room Limalimo ecolodge, run in conjunction with the African Wildlife Foundation in order to help preserve the landscape and its endemic wildlife, while at the same time providing valuable income to local communities. Located thousands of feet above the Simien Escarpment, at one of the most stunning viewpoints of the entire park, the lodge is decorated in traditional Ethiopian style and offers delicious home-made food, yoga, massage and the chance to meet with the local villagers and learn more about their way of life: *www.limalimolodge.com*

WHILE YOU'RE THERE: Visit the rock-hewn churches of Lalibela, 285 miles to the south. Chiselled directly from the volcanic rock beds surrounding the town, these eleven 13th-century buildings are a true wonder of the world and one of the great architectural masterpieces of Africa: *www.ethiopia.travel*

TOUBKAL NATIONAL PARK, MOROCCO

Morocco is a place that consumes the senses: fresh tagines smoking by the roadside, ancient citadels, flowers in the

Sahara, the muezzin call to prayer echoing through fields of parched and brittle wheat. It has inspired painters, poets and musicians for centuries; it oozes artistry from every delicately carved facade, mosaic and cup of sweet mint tea. Morocco isn't a destination, it's a land of enchantment, sensuality and wonder.

All roads pass through Marrakesh, one of the world's most dazzling cities. There are many highlights: the winding labyrinth of its souks; the ancient Medina, Djemaa el-Fna, its main square, at night. A circus of snake charmers, dancers, musicians and fortune-tellers, steam sizzling from fresh barbeques all around.

But just 50 miles to the south is another world entirely. Away from the bustle of the city, the High Atlas Mountains rise from the plains north the Sahara like a sleeping colossus, crossing the entire country from the Atlantic coast, in the south-west, to the Algerian border, in the north-east. At their heart, is Toubkal National Park, 147 square miles of rugged mountain scenery and rural Moroccan culture, framed by the pyramidal summit of Mount, or Jbel, Toubkal itself, 13,671 feet tall, like the tip of a stone scimitar, jagged and shouldered in snow.

Most people come to stand on its summit, the second highest peak on the continent, after Kilimanjaro. The hike up usually takes between two to four days, with various routes on offer, but the last night is always spent at a mountain refuge a few hours from the summit, meaning you rise in the dark, hike by moonlight and stand on the roof of North Africa for the sunrise. The views are breathtaking: a blaze of red and deep ochre, canyons filled with cherry blossoms, knuckle edge ridges that disappear in endless slow rows, like mountain waves rolling into the shimmering heat of the horizon. Stand here and it's the enormity of Africa that strikes you. The High Atlases are the guardians of the Sahara. Look south, over the last distant peaks of this range, and there is nothing but a sea of sand, and then the great plains of Africa, for thousands of miles.

Outside of the trekking, there are many sights to see: the walled city of Taroudant, built in the 16th century, just a short drive from the park; the Kasbah Aït Benhaddou, the best-preserved Kasbah in the country, used in films such as *Lawrence of Arabia* and *Gladiator*; Asni, one of the best rural markets in the country, on the road in from Marrakesh; Imlil, the beautiful High Atlas village that serves as the most popular base for the park.

But wherever you go, what you'll remember, the real wonders of Toubkal National Park are the Berbers. Theirs is the traditional rural Morocco that few tourists get to see. Simple stone houses held together with a mixture of mud, salt and chaff from the fields; shepherds herding their flock to nearby watering holes; a donkey laden with alfalfa, slumped in the shade of a fig tree. People here live the old ways, cooking in communal outdoor ovens, milling grain by mule, shaking olives from centuries-old family trees to hand press into delicious oil.

The Berbers are the indigenous people of Morocco. They have lived in these mountains, and elsewhere in North Africa, for at least the last 5,000 years. The name Berber derives from the Latin *Barbari*, or barbarians, a title given to them almost 2,000 years ago by invading Roman armies who were repeatedly attacked by a race of fiercely independent tribes that refused to be subjugated. But despite their reputation, the modern-day descendants of those warriors – the Imazighen, as they prefer to call themselves – are a disarmingly gentle and welcoming people. Come here and you live as they do: staying overnight in their villages, sleeping on simple hand-woven carpets in their homes; you share mint tea with them, cous cous and lamb tagine, scooped up with fresh baked bread; you go to their markets, wilder and more visceral than the tourist souks of the city: stalls of honey and freshly toasted almonds alongside butchered sheep; a potter's wheel spinning clay; chickens and wild dogs roaming free. It's like stepping back in time.

But that's why it's so important too. Here, in the foothills of the Atlas Mountains we have a glimpse of a North African way of life that has remained unchanged for centuries. It soaks into your skin, that gentleness, that pride, that generosity of spirit. The symbol of the Berbers is a man holding his arms to the sky, a free man, a man who refuses to be conquered. That's how Toubkal makes you feel: elevated, enchanted, filled with sensuality and wonder, unstoppable, unconquerable, alive.

WHERE: Central western Morocco, 50 miles south of Marrakesh. The nearest town, and most common gateway to the park, is Imlil: *www.visitmorocco.com*

DON'T MISS: Spending the night in a Berber village. Most trekking companies will use local villages as base camps; the best use local Berber guides too with the opportunity to stay overnight in local family homes – valuable income for the village and a rare insight into a remarkable way of life. Climbing Toubkal is a Berber owned and operated tour company based in Imlil (*www.climbingtoubkal.com*) or check *https://www.responsibletravel.com/holidays/morocco* for various well-vetted options.

TOP TIP: If you can afford it spend a few nights at the Kasbah du Toubkal, in Imlil. This award-winning traditional lodge,

one of National Geographic's celebrated 'unique lodges of the world' collection, is the perfect base for exploring the park with sumptuous food, a superb Hamman and one of the best rooftop views in Africa: *www.kasbahdutoubkal.com*

WHILE YOU'RE THERE: Marrakesh is a must: make sure to spend at least two days exploring the city before venturing into the park. But consider a few days relaxing in Essaouira at the end too. This delightful white-washed beach resort, with excellent surf and gorgeous blue-shuttered houses, is the essence of Moroccan seaside romance: chic dining, old hippy hang outs (Jimi Hendrix lived here for a while in the 60s) and some of the best traditional music, art and culture in the country: *www.essaouira.nu*

ASIA

SAGARMATHA NATIONAL PARK, NEPAL

Sagarmatha National Park is the home of Mount Everest. The Sherpas, who have lived here for centuries, call her Chomolungma, Tibetan for 'Goddess Mother of the World'. The Nepalese call her 'Peak of Heaven'. Whichever name you use, one thing's for certain: Everest is more than a mountain – it's a symbol of the human spirit for adventure and exploration. To stand upon its summit is not just foolish vanity; it is the will to walk among the gods. George Mallory, who lost his life in 1924, attempting to be the first person to make it to the top, said we climb it 'because it's there';

we climb it because to look into the abyss, to know our own fragile mortality, but still dare to cross that dark boundary, is what makes us human and what has carried us so far.

At 29,035 feet, it is the tallest mountain on Earth – high enough to touch the edge of the jet stream. From the tip of its pyramidal like peak, the darkness beyond the stratosphere reveals itself like a dawning night. Temperatures never rise above freezing, even in summer, and can suddenly plummet to minus 76 degrees Fahrenheit, cold enough to lose an exposed piece of skin in minutes. Winds gust at 175 miles per hour. Avalanches rain on all sides. Breathing is near impossible.

But still people climb it. The first successful attempt was by Sir Edmund Hillary and Tenzing Norgay, on 29 May 1953. Since then there have been some incredible ascents. In 1978, Reinhold Messner became the first person to climb Everest without supplemental oxygen – a feat that was thought biologically impossible at the time. Two years later he did it again, this time solo. The youngest to make it to the summit is thirteen-year-old Jordan Romero, from America; the oldest, 80-year-old Yuichiro Miura, from Japan. In 1990, Tim Macartney-Snape travelled unaided from sea-level, at the Bay of Bengal, to the top of Mount Everest. And then six years later, Goran Kropp topped this, cycling all the way from his home in Sweden to base camp, ascending Everest, and then cycling home. Everest has now been snowboarded, skied and paraglided over, there's even been a wedding on top (talk about cold feet).

But the greatest accomplishments of all are performed by the Sherpas, year in and year out. These ethnic Tibetans, who migrated here over 500 years ago, possess a unique physiology, a result of centuries living at altitude, which allows them to absorb oxygen quicker at higher elevations,

Photo: Faj2525

perfectly adapting them to life on the roof of the world. Because of that, many of them work as porters and guides, assisting groups of mountaineers to the summit of Everest and other peaks in the park. It's a sight to see: while we struggle and gasp for breath, they haul load after load with seeming ease.

But even more important is the way they get there. For the Sherpas, Chomolungma is sacred. When they climb her, they must ask for permission first – performing the Puja, in which all members of the team leave offerings and pay homage to the mountain, asking for her grace to return safely to their families. It is typical of these peaceful, Buddhist people – rather than conquer the mountain, as we in the West do, they ask for communion instead.

Spending time with them is an integral part of any trip to Sagarmatha National Park. Trek to Everest Base Camp, a two-week hike and one of the most popular routes in the park, or to the Gokyo Lakes, another highlight, and you will stay in their tea houses and homes along the way, eating hearty bowls of Tibetan stew, sharing bottles of maize beer and learning about their unique mountain culture.

That's the true joy of Sagarmatha National Park. To see the world's highest peak is a dazzling, humbling experience; to dare to walk upon its slopes, one of the world's great adventures. But you don't need to be a superhuman, or risk your life, to soak up the magic of the Himalayas. These are the world's most magnificent mountains; the highest peaks on the planet, deep-glacier valleys, dotted with farms and villages, monasteries on the mountain, prayer flags fluttering in the breeze. There are treks for all levels and abilities, as well as places to simply sit and contemplate the breathtaking enormity of the scenery all around. Often, that is enough. To stand on the highest point on the planet is life changing, but just being here, surrounded by such natural grandeur, such kindness and simplicity, is to walk among the gods still.

WHERE: Eastern Nepal. The nearest town is Namche Bazaar, a spectacular Sherpa community two days walk from Lukla. Flights to Lukla leave from Kathmandu daily:
www.sagarmathanationalpark.gov.np
www.welcomenepal.com

DON'T MISS: The spectacular Tengboche Monastery, one of the most stunning monasteries in all of Nepal, framed by the incredible backdrop of Mt. Ama Dablam. Located along the trek to Everest Base Camp, it is also one of the best spots from which to photograph the mountain itself – get there early to avoid clouds for the best shot.

TOP TIP: If you want to know what it feels like to stand on the tallest mountain of the world, without having to risk your neck getting there, check out Sólfar Studios' *Everest VR* – a nerve-jangling virtual reality ascent from Base Camp to the summit that has proved too realistic for some early reviewers to handle: *www.solfar.com/everest-vr*

WHILE YOU'RE THERE: See a completely different side to Nepal at Chitwan National Park, set deep in the jungle of Southern Nepal – one of the best wildlife-viewing parks in Asia, filled with rhinos, monkeys, elephants and more:
www.chitwannationalpark.gov.np

JIUZHAI VALLEY NATIONAL PARK, CHINA

The Jiuzhai Valley is China's most treasured national park. Located in the Min Shan mountains of Northern Sichuan, on the edge of the Tibetan Plateau, a vast high plain bordered by the tallest peaks of the planet on all sides, Jiuzhaigou, as it's also known, is, quite simply, one of the most beautiful places on Earth. Meaning 'Nine Village Valley', the park is named after nine traditional Tibetan villages, scattered throughout the region, many of which date back thousands of years and still keep the traditions of their ancient, spiritual culture alive – this isn't just one of China's most celebrated landscapes, it's an emblem of the Tibetan people too, a fragment of their great, exiled civilisation.

But its lakes are the star. Pure turquoise waters, as clear as glass; blue rivers like melted sapphires; waterfalls spilling down from limestone terraces; purple pools, azure streams. Formed from a twenty-mile Y-shaped valley, it is said once you have seen the lakes of the Jiuzhai Valley, there is no need to gaze upon water again, nothing could ever compare. Science will tell you that it is an abundance of calcium carbonate, and other mineral deposits that has blessed them with such astonishing colour. But the legends say something different, that they were formed when a young demigod, Dage, besotted with love, bestowed a gift upon the goddess Woluo Semo – a mirror made of pure wind – which was destroyed by a jealous demon, smashing it into 114 pieces that fell to Earth and formed the sparkling lakes we see today. Whatever you believe, this is a place of fables and fairy tales, rainbows and dreams, too bright and vivid, surely, to be the work of mere minerals alone.

The main gorge, the stem of the Y, is the Shu Zheng Valley,

home of the magnificent Shu Zheng Lakes, nineteen pure blue pools, interconnected by a series of cobalt rivers and rushing waterfalls, hundreds of individual streams pouring over the rocks like strands of silk all around. Nearby is Reed Lake, covered in a carpet of thick foliage, blue waterways cutting through the greenery like paint swirling in a pot. At its far end is the imposing Jia Wu sacred mountain, where the ruins of an ancient Buddhist pagoda still serve as an altar for the local Tibetan people today, who perform religious ceremonies and seek blessings from the divine waters here.

Branching to the left is the Zechawa Valley, home of Long Lake, the park's biggest, indigo water surrounded by snow-capped peaks; and the spectacular Five Coloured Pond, where a unique combination of travertine sedimentation and algae has created a kaleidoscope of bright blue, green, purple, yellow and red water – like watching a rainbow transformed to a stream.

Running parallel is the Rize Valley, where the Nuo Ri Waterfall, the largest travertine waterfall in the world, rushes beside the Five Flower Lake, dazzling underwater hues mixing with the cerulean waters like paint swirling in a crystal sea. But perhaps most special of all is Panda Lake. The Jiuzhai Valley is one of the few habitats in the world that supports the giant panda. At one time, they were prolific, coming down to the waters here to drink and swim, but deforestation has forced them to venture higher into the mountains in search of bamboo to feed and sightings, unfortunately, are increasingly rare. Today only 2,000 are left in the wild.

But they're not the only animal here: the park supports a myriad of wildlife from red pandas and Asiatic black bears to grey wolves and, perhaps favourite of all, the Sichuan

golden monkey, found only in these mountains, with red-orange coats and a face as blue as the lakes they call home.

There's more than just natural beauty too. The nine villages of the valley are home to roughly 1,000 people. Shu Zheng village is the most popular, with a golden *dagoba* temple in its centre and numerous traditional houses and shops. Ze Cha Wa and Hey Li are beautiful too, doors and windows decorated in bright patterns. The others are harder to access but better for it, less commercial and more authentic, especially in the Zharu Valley, home of the spectacular Zharu Monastery, a complex of religious halls, tea rooms and quarters for working lamas, set high in the mountains, with a golden wheel at its entrance, symbolising the cyclical transformation of life and death.

Nearby, is the sacred Zha Yi Zha Ga, the Tibetan king of all mountains, rising nearly 15,000 feet to the sky, with a large statue of the Buddha guarding its entrance. On the 15th of every month, this holy peak is encircled by devout Benbo Tibetan pilgrims as part of a ritual ceremony. It's a hard and steep hike, but filled with stunning views throughout. Walk these trails and the traditional Tibetan culture of the park truly comes alive: yak butter tea, barley wine and *tsampa*; long banners printed with sacred text, strung out in the breeze because, it is believed, the wind will set the prayers free.

Perhaps it will. Tibetan culture today is under threat from a dominant Chinese ideology. Although the Chinese claim sovereignty over Tibet, which they used to justify their 1950 invasion and subsequent occupation of the country, most Tibetans, including their spiritual leader, the Dalai Lama, dispute this claim. Since that occupation, Tibetan culture and the Tibetan people have been marginalised or worse – with any expression of their culture, whether religious or symbolic, strictly prohibited.

When you come here, remember them. The Jiuzhai Valley is one of the most aesthetically beautiful landscapes on Earth, a place filled with the wonder of nature in all its unbounded colour and majesty. For the Tibetans, that majesty, these mountains, lakes and rivers, are part of their soul too. Jiuzhai Valley National Park is one of the last bastions of their traditional way of life, a prayer flag flickering in the storm. But the wind is listening and their flags are standing strong.

WHERE: Northern Sichuan, Aba Tibetan and Qiang Autonomous Prefecture, South-west China. There are numerous hotels around the park entrance to use as a base. Regular flights, or (eight–ten-hour) bus journeys depart from Chengu: *www.jiuzhai.com*

DON'T MISS: Taking the three-day guided hike around the Zha Yi Zha Ga Sacred Mountain, the best way to experience the authentic Tibetan culture of the region and the only way to sleep in the park itself, camping out in local villages each night: *www.jiuzhai.com/language/english/ecotourism.html*

TOP TIP: The most photogenic time to visit is September and October, when the leaves change colour and contrast dramatically with the blue-green lakes. But it's also the busiest time. Avoid some of the crowds by walking between the main sites instead of taking the tourist bus. There is a network of excellent wood platforms that connect each of the lakes, and while the main viewpoints may be crowded, you'll have the parts in between all to yourself.

WHILE YOU'RE THERE: Spend a day in Huanglong National Park, just to the south – another spectacular valley filled with multi-coloured travertine lakes, waterfalls and wild forests on all sides: *www.chinadiscovery.com/sichuan/ jiuzhaigou/huanglong-national-park.html*

JIGME DORJI NATIONAL PARK, BHUTAN

Bhutan is the last of the great Himalayan kingdoms. Still largely untouched by the outside world, shrouded in mystery and magic, this Buddhist country, hidden deep in the mountains for centuries, is like nowhere else on Earth. It is the only carbon-negative country on the planet – they actually remove more CO_2 from the atmosphere than they put in. They are also the only country to measure progress by Gross National Happiness, not Gross National Product – because, according to official statements, the rich are not always happy, but the happy generally consider themselves to be rich. The people live in harmony with the natural world. They are embracing modernity at a sustainable pace. The culture is strong. Bhutan is, quite possibly, the most enlightened place on Earth.

But it's easier to be enlightened when you live where they do. Druk Yul, as it's known by its people, 'The Land of the Fire Dragon', is located in the Eastern Himalayas, sandwiched between China, Northern India and Tibet, and ringed by the world's highest peaks. Mountains crowned in snow rise like a veil of stone all around, emerald rivers flow into sharp gorges and sparkling, cobalt lakes, wildflowers and thick primeval forest dab the foothills in lush colour. This is the Himalayas at their most pristine. There is a vitality here, an energy, that comes from the land, from the scale, from knowing how small we are compared to it, yet how inextricably intertwined with it we still are.

But it's the culture that makes Bhutan truly inspiring. For centuries, it was unknown by most of the world, and it still has that feel today. Deeply religious, Buddhist architecture dominates the landscape, from the enormous white-washed Dzongs (towering fortress-like buildings which surround complexes of temples inside), to monasteries perched precariously on rocky cliffs, clinging to the steep slopes like precious mountain flowers. But this is no museum. Although the Bhutanese are slowly adopting many aspects of the modern world, they are not doing so at the expense of their heritage. Bhutanese culture is a living, thriving thing.

It begins with the traditional dress, still worn by most people today: bright flowing kimono-like robes, called Gho, for the men, and the Kira, a long silky dress, embroidered with vibrant patterns of yellow, purple, turquoise and red, for the women. Traditional arts and crafts are still practised too: weaving with bamboo and cane, basket-making and ceramics; beautifully detailed patterns and rich carvings adorning every religious facade. But it's the festivals that really stand out. Religious celebrations, called Tshechus, are held at villages and temples throughout the year, bringing the entire community together to celebrate with traditional masked dances, songs and music – they are the ultimate expression of Bhutanese culture: all strands – the beliefs, artistry and breathtaking scenery, woven together as one.

As for the national park, Jigme Dorji is a wonderland. Most people come for the trekking. The best in the world is here: soaring up mountain peaks, through glacier ice-fields and sun-dappled forests of oak, hemlock and Himalayan yew. One of the most popular is the eight-day Jomolhari Trek, travelling from the ruined Drukgyal Dzong, above the Paro Valley, then

Photo: A. J. T. Johnsingh, WWF-India and NCF

skirting the Tibetan border on a high ridge, overlooking the capital Thimphu, to the base of the sacred Jomolhari peak itself. Passing through villages and farms along the way, sharing stories and spicy plates of traditional home-cooked food – hiking simply doesn't get any better than this.

Elsewhere in the park there are hot springs, the Gasa Tsachu – renowned for their therapeutic properties, used by locals and tourists alike; the 17th-century Cheri Monastery, the first monastic seat of Bhutan, high on a lush forest hill overlooking the Wangchu River; and remote villages, which can only be reached on foot and where the lives of people have changed imperceptibly in centuries, herding yaks and harvesting medicinal plants to trade.

But its most famous resident you are almost guaranteed never to see. The elusive snow leopard, known as 'the ghost of the mountains', one of the hardest animals in the world to see in the wild, makes its home here, feeding on yak and blue sheep, striking from the shadows and disappearing silently again without a trace. Recent studies indicate that there are likely to be 31 of these big cats in the park, making Jigme Dorji the best place in the world to catch a glimpse of one, if you're lucky, or more likely, of their tracks, as they watch you pass by in perfect stillness, hidden somewhere up there in the peaks, camouflaged against the frosty ground.

The snow leopard is a good metaphor for Bhutan too. As the modern world races past, this lost Himalayan kingdom watches silently on, hidden in the mountains, adopting what it needs, but losing nothing for it, seeking happiness over wealth, a life lived in harmony with the elements, leaving only footprints that fade with the seasons and the first snows of winter's storm.

WHERE: North-west Bhutan. The nearby capital of Thimphu

is often used as a starting point for further explorations: *www.tourism.gov.bt*

DON'T MISS: Bhutan's most famous hike, just a couple of hours west of Thimphu: the spectacular trek to Taktshang Goempa (Tiger's Nest) monastery, which clings to the sheer edge of a cliff, 3,000 feet above the Paro Valley – Bhutan's most iconic landmark:
www.tourism.gov.bt/contact/taktsang-lhakhang-2

TOP TIP: Time your visit with Bhutan's biggest Tshechu festival, held in the capital Thimphu every year – one of the most spectacular cultural events in the entire country, attended by thousands of locals and tourists alike. The exact dates vary, but it's usually held around September. Check website for details: *www.tourism.gov.bt*

WHILE YOU'RE THERE: Visit Jigme Singye Wangchuck National Park, in the central part of the country – one of the largest tracts of undisturbed forests in the Himalayas, filled with red pandas, golden langurs, rare clouded leopards and the majestic Royal Bengal Tiger: *www.tourism.gov.bt/central-bhutan/jigme-singye-wangchuck-national-park*

RANTHAMBORE NATIONAL PARK, INDIA

Ranthambore National Park, in Northern India, is one of the best places in the world to see tigers in the wild. Fierce, powerful beasts, renowned for their strength and cunning, they were once feared throughout the land. Now they are a treasure of the country, a symbol of wild India, its gracefulness, sensuality and colour.

But they are in need of protection. Bengal tigers used to roam vast ranges of the continent. At the turn of the 20th century there were thought to have been between 20,000 and 40,000 in the wild. Now less than 3,000 remain – and poaching, in many places, as well as loss of habitat, are constant threats. Not here. Ranthambore is the cornerstone of India's tiger conservation programme, Project Tiger; and in recent years there has been a cautious resurgence in numbers. But problems still persist. As populations across the country continue to be threatened, coming here, helping to fund anti-poaching initiatives and prove a sustainable business model for the country and local communities alike, may be the only way to save them.

But even though the cats are the big draw, they are only part of the park's appeal. Ranthambore was the former hunting ground of the Maharajas, or great kings, the princely rulers of Rajasthan who lived in almost unimaginable splendour until their titles, and more importantly their government pocket money, was cut off in 1971. Tales of their opulence are legendary: diamond-studded miniature train sets to ferry the after-dinner port around the dining table; a silver encrusted bed with life-size moveable bronze statues of fanning, fawning women; the Patiala Necklace, the largest single piece ever made by Cartier, adorned with a staggering 2,930 diamonds and weighing in at almost 1,000 carats.

Much of that history, although now faded from its original grandeur, is still evident in the park today: the ancient palace ruins of Raj Bagh, elaborate domes, minarets and arches slowly being consumed by the jungle; the resplendent Nahargarh, their former hunting palace (now a luxury hotel), surrounded by a formal Mughal garden and 16th-century fortress; everywhere you look ancient ruins are scattered, like jewels, throughout the forest.

But the most famous, and beautiful, part of the park's heritage is Ranthambore Fort. Constructed in the mid-10th century, this enormous walled complex of temples, palaces and domed pavilions, built on a rocky outcrop 700 feet above the forest plains, was one of the most formidable defensive strongholds of the time, controlling the important trade routes between north and central India. One of six such hill forts in the region, all inscribed by UNESCO, together they form one of the most important legacies of India's rich artistic culture.

But that's just the start. What makes Ranthambore one of the greatest national parks in the world is not just what's on offer within its boundaries, but what's nearby. India is a place that floods the senses: fresh curry sizzling on the streets; Hindu prayers by candlelight; the madness of the city; the temple at dawn. There are many special regions, but Rajasthan, Ranthambore's province, is truly special: home of Jaipur, the fabled Pink City, the bazaars of Udaipur and the magnificent Taj Mahal, the most breathtakingly beautiful building the world has ever seen. When you come to Ranthambore National Park, you come for the whole experience: the lost world of the Maharajas, the majestic hill forts, the temples, the incense, the chanting, the colour. India is a place of overwhelming sensuality and grace. No wonder the tiger is its national treasure, no other animal could match such raw splendour, strength and style. Look one in the eyes and you will find the heart of India looking back.

WHERE: Rajasthan, Northern India, just over 100 miles south of Jaipur. The nearest town is Sawai Madhopur: *www.ranthamborenationalpark.com*

Photo: Wiki-arun

DON'T MISS: Time your visit with the Holi Festival, the Hindu Festival of Colour, when the entire country takes to the streets in what is effectively one giant paint fight. Expect to celebrate all day, all night and get covered from head to toe in brightly coloured *gulal* powder. Jaipur and Agra, both near Ranthambore National Park, hold two of the biggest celebrations in the country. The exact date changes each year, but is usually held sometime from the end of February to early March. Check website for details: *www.holifestival.com*

TOP TIP: For the best chance of spotting tigers allow a few days. The park is split up into zones, with guests randomly assigned which area of the park they will be exploring that day. Zones 2–5 are usually the best for spotting tigers.

WHILE YOU'RE THERE: Plan on seeing Rajasthan's main sites: Taj Mahal, Jaipur and more. But consider timing your visit with the Pushkar Camel Fair too, less than 100 miles from Jaipur. Usually held at the end of October or early November, this is one of India's most colourful annual festivals, with an incredible array of cultural celebrations, competitions, camel races and more: *www.pushkarcamelfair.com*

FUJI-HAKONE-IZU NATIONAL PARK, JAPAN

Mount Fuji is the perfect mountain. A near-flawless cone, symmetrical on all sides, with a crown of snow most of the year, Fuji-san, as it's known in Japan, isn't so much a natural wonder as a work of art. Perhaps, that's not surprising: this 12,388-foot-high stratovolcano (which is still active, last erupting in 1707 when it rained ash on the city of Tokyo, just 62 miles to the east) has inspired Japanese painters and poets for centuries. There is no other place in the country that represents this proudly traditional island better. Mount Fuji is the soul of the Japanese people themselves.

Fuji-san has been worshipped for thousands of years. Named after the Buddhist fire goddess, Fuchi, and considered sacred by Japan's indigenous Shinto faith (a shrine to the Shinto goddess Sengen-Sama is on its summit as well as numerous others along its slope and base), this is the most revered of Japan's three holy mountains, considered to be an embodiment of the very spirit of nature itself. For many, it was a gateway to enlightenment too. In the 12th century, the slopes of Fuji-san were the site of Buddhist ascetic, or Shugendō, training, in which practitioners would perform ritual pilgrimage ascents and descents, stopping to worship at various sacred sites along the way – many of which still exist. For them, spiritual awakening was attained through immersion in the natural world. Mount Fuji was their church; her paths their altar; each step a prayer uttered to the mountain itself.

It's a tradition that continues to this day. Hundreds of thousands make it to the top each year. But it's not easy. The full climb is steep and takes roughly eight hours, though there are ten stations, or mountain refuges, along the way, which provide rest and refreshment. One popular option is to take the bus to the 5th station (between 4,593 and 7,874 feet up) and begin from there, roughly halving the length of the hike. Even better, book a bed in one of the refuges near the top, then get up in the dark and watch dawn break over the 'Land of the Rising Sun' – a view shared by pilgrims and monks for thousands of years: volcanic red scree circling the 1,600-foot-wide caldera, the world disappearing in misty blue dawn below.

The mountain is, of course, the main attraction but there are other highlights too. The Five Lakes region, a series of natural pools that reflect the mountain in perfect symmetry, offers some of the best opportunities for photographers, especially in spring when cherry blossom blooms all around. Cruises on the lakes are also popular, as is a visit to the 8th-century Fujiyoshida Sengen Shrine, lined with a towering forest of ancient cedar trees, and the Fujisan Sengen Shrine, the most important shrine of the region and the traditional starting point for pilgrimages up the mountain.

Also in the park, on the south-eastern edge, is Hakone, one of the country's most popular hot spring resorts. Known as *onsen* in Japan, these natural mineral bathing pools have been an important part of Japanese culture for centuries and have strict rules and etiquette around them. Far more than a simple soak, an *onsen* is a kind of purification ceremony and a direct way to connect with traditional Japanese culture and heritage. The perfect end to a day on the mountain.

And who knows: perhaps, some of that enlightenment those Shugendō monks were seeking will rub off on you too. It's an intriguing idea. Ninety nine per cent of our genetic history has been spent intimately connected to nature. It's part of who we are. Perhaps if enlightenment is to be found anywhere, it's outside of us, not within. Mount Fuji is a good place to start looking.

WHERE: Yamanashi, Kanagawa and Shizuoka Prefectures, 62 miles west of Tokyo. The town of Hakone, within the national park itself, is a good base: *www.env.go.jp/en/nature/ nps/park/fujihakone/index.html*

DON'T MISS: Watching the sunrise from the summit of Mount Fuji. Hike up the Fujinomiya Trail the afternoon before. This is the most westerly path up the mountain and offers the best sunset views, as well as the fewest crowds (a relative thing, Mount Fuji is always busy). Book a bed in one of the nine mountain huts along this route (there are 44 in total, if you choose one of the other paths) and then wake up two hours before sunrise to finish the hike to the top. The official climbing season is July and August – avoid school and public holidays. Book well in advance: *www.jnto. go.jp/eng/arrange/travel/practical/pdf/Mt.Hut_Mt.Fuji.pdf*

TOP TIP: If you don't plan on climbing Mount Fuji, avoid the summer: the crowds are huge and the mountain, many would say, is less photogenic without its dusting of snow on top. For the best views, and photographs, come cherry blossom season instead, which usually peaks around mid-April. Be aware, too, that the mountain is often covered in clouds – especially in summer. Colder temperatures usually bring clearer skies, but factor in an extra couple of days to avoid disappointment. A list of good cherry blossom–Mount Fuji viewpoints can be found here: *www.japan-guide.com/e/e6920.html*

WHILE YOU'RE THERE: Tokyo is just an hour away by train and should be combined with any trip to Fuji-Hakone-Izu National Park. But, if you're interested in finding out more about Shugendō, or traditional Japanese Shintoism, then head to the Kii Peninsula, south of Kyoto to hike the Kumano Kodō. This spectacular 54-mile pilgrimage route, which has been walked by emperors and peasants alike for more than a thousand years, links together some of the country's best history and mountain scenery. There are various options, but Oku Japan is one of the best, offering excellent guided and self-guided trips staying in traditional Japanese *ryokans* along the way: *www.okujapan.com*

KOMODO NATIONAL PARK, INDONESIA

Komodo National Park, in Indonesia, is the home of the largest lizard on the planet. Reaching up to ten feet long, and weighing more than 300 pounds, with razor-sharp claws and jaws that can devour 80 per cent of their body weight in a single sitting, the Komodo Dragon is the stuff of nightmares. Where other wildlife encounters elicit a sense of deep connection and awe, Komodo Dragons fill us with primal fear. They are a relic from another eon, a myth made real, the shadow under your bed. Komodo Dragons remind us of a time, not so long ago, when monsters ruled the Earth and humans ran scared from their path.

We haven't known about them for long. Although legends of colossal-size lizards, real-life dragons, had floated on the waves with sailors for centuries, they weren't officially discovered by Western science until 1910, when whispers of a 'land crocodile', or 'Ora', as the local islanders call them, reached a nearby Dutch colony. But it wasn't until 1926, when a handsome young American socialite by the name of William Douglas Burden decided to catch one for himself, that their infamy truly spread. He sailed for Komodo Island, in what is now the heart of the national park, with his wife and a cameraman, set traps, caught two live specimens and returned a hero. That incredible story inspired the imagination of his good friend, Merian Cooper, who would go on to produce a remarkably similar tale about another oversized beast, also captured from an exotic island and also put on display – this one, though, about a gorilla: King Kong. Indeed, in the original script (until budgets and limitations on special effects changed his plans) Cooper had him fighting none other than a Komodo Dragon itself.

And although the word dragon is a nickname, many people believe that the Komodos may have been the real-life inspiration for the dragons of our myths, a figure that has appeared in legends and fairy tales, in one form or another, in almost every country of the world. Proving this was Burden's true hope for the mission, writing in his book *Dragon Lizards of Komodo*: 'Dragon stories must originally have been founded on fact, that is, on some beast that actually lives, a giant carnivorous lizard, perhaps, whose size and strength and voracious habits were such as properly to impress the mind of primitive man.'

For years serious scientists thought it unlikely. The Komodo Dragons exist in this one remote island chain and nowhere else in the world. Their numbers are relatively small. That they could have influenced global culture to such a degree seems far-fetched. But new evidence may prove Burden correct. A recent study of fossil records shows that Indonesia's giant lizards were actually once part of a much larger distribution of related species, that evolved in Australia about 4 million years ago (much later than the last dinosaur) and then spread out across the region. Far from an anomaly, which had been the prevailing theory to date, super-sized lizards were once the norm; and Komodos weren't even the big boys, their frames actually proving relatively small compared to the fossils found of some others, including the eighteen-foot giant Megalania. It turns out, dragons really did walk the Earth; the Komodos are just all that's left.

And although they don't breathe fire, they do have bad breath. Komodo Dragons are fast, able to sprint up to thirteen miles per hour to catch their prey, but they're

Photo: Jon Chia

smart too, preferring to wait in ambush for unsuspecting passers-by – preferably deer, but also water buffalo, pig, monkeys and other small mammals. All they need is one bite. Their saliva is laden with over 50 strains of bacteria, as well as venom secreted from glands inside their jaws – even a scratch is enough to cause blood poisoning and gradual loss of consciousness or death in their prey. Rather than risk their own scaly skin, the Komodo simply strikes once and then stalks their victim, slowly watching them stumble, succumb to the poison, and die.

But dragons aren't the only reason to visit. Made up of three main islands, Komodo, Rinca and Padar, the scenery here is spectacular – Burden called it 'haunting, mysterious'; worthy of inspiration for King Kong's exotic hideaway for sure. Lush volcanic mountains rise straight from the sea in a dazzle of primary colours, blue and green, lined by white sand beaches along the shore. The ocean teems with dolphins, manta rays, turtles, whales and some of the brightest coral you'll ever see. Nearby, there are traditional villages; about 4,000 people live here in all – many of whom still tell legends of the Komodos as the 'Dragon Princess', a benign creature descended from a god, not an enemy to be feared.

But for us, it's different. Dragons may be the stuff of myths, an obstacle the hero must overcome, a shadow, a fear personified. Here they're real. Never mind the beauty of their dark, multi-hued scales, nor the fact that attacks on humans are rare. In our minds, they are monsters. They are the reason you pull the blanket over your head in the dark of night. Come and see them if you dare.

WHERE: The centre of the Indonesian archipelago, between the islands of Sumbawa and Flores. Flights leave daily from Bali. Check website for details: *www.floreskomodo.com*

DON'T MISS: Snorkelling and scuba-diving in the reefs around the park, one of the best places in the world for doing so. Don't worry: no water dragons here.

TOP TIP: December is the best time for viewing Komodo Dragons in the park. July and August is the mating season, when the dragons can be more aggressive. September to November is the nesting season, when they can be harder to spot.

WHILE YOU'RE THERE: Visit Kelimutu National Park, on the neighbouring island of Flores. It's famous for its multicoloured lakes and it set within a spectacular landscape of flooded calderas and sharp jungle peaks:
www.florestourism.com

YALA NATIONAL PARK, SRI LANKA

Yala National Park, in South-east Sri Lanka, is the best place in the world to see leopards in the wild. These elusive animals, which are notoriously hard to spot, are so abundant here (statistically about two and a half for every square mile), that sightings, while never guaranteed, are more likely than not. They are remarkable creatures: astoundingly strong (pound for pound they can lift more than any other big cat), lightning fast (they can run up to 36 miles per hour) and supremely agile (able to jump an astonishing twelve feet vertically and twenty feet horizontally). They are, in many ways, the perfect predator. But it is, perhaps, their elegance that catches the eye the most. Leopards have style, dark

Photo: Michael Gunther

rosettes spotting their soft, light coats and a gracefulness of movement rarely rivalled in the animal kingdom. Seeing one in the wild should be on the bucket list of any wildlife fan. But you'll see far more than that while you're here.

Yala is Sri Lanka's premier national park – 378 square miles of this incredible little island's most diverse and wildlife-rich scenery, from thick jungle and rocky plains to freshwater lakes, rivers and golden beaches along the shore. The park is split into five blocks, or areas, each with their own character. The southern region, blocks 1 and 2, are the most popular – wide open grasslands that offer the best visibility and the most leopards, usually found perfectly camouflaged in the high branches of a tree, but occasionally on the chase: stalking wild boar and spotted deer, pouncing from the shadows on unsuspecting prey. Sand dunes and crashing surf frame the far southern boundaries, while inland, mangroves, wetland and lagoons puncture the arid ground with pools of life-giving water that teem with water buffaloes, crocodiles and Yala's highest concentration of birdlife.

Blocks 3, 4 and 5 make up the northern aspect of the park. The landscape is wilder here, more overgrown. Tourist safaris are less common, meaning the animals are wary and harder to spot. But it's worth the effort. Deep into these mature forests are Sri Lanka's largest population of Indian elephants: smart, playful animals, that congregate around watering holes – the highlight of many a visit.

Coming here, in many ways, is comparable to an African safari – sunrise and sundown bush drives, wildlife on every bend. But among the sambar deers and jackals, the sloth bears and leopards peering through the trees, there are also the remnants of Sri Lanka's rich and colourful past. Centuries ago, Yala was the height of a thriving civilisation, the ancient Sinhalese Kingdom of Ruhuna, and an echo of that past life still remains. Ruined granaries, old stone watering tanks, and dome-shaped shrines with ancient relics inside are peppered throughout the land. In the north-east, the enormous Magul Maha Viharaya temple complex, built to celebrate the marriage of King Kavan-Tissa to Vihara Maha Devi in the 2nd century BC, overflows with intricately carved moonstones, plinths and statues. In the South, the pilgrimage town of Kataragama, which has been sacred to Buddhists, Hindus, Muslims and Christians alike for thousands of years, is filled with mosques, Tamil shrines and a Bo tree, purportedly grown from the sapling of the Bodhi tree under which Gotama Buddha attained enlightenment, all side by side.

But the highlight is Sithulpawwa. Perched on the edge of a colossal 400-foot-tall rock, this 2,000-year-old Buddhist temple, which means 'the hill of the quiet mind', was once the home of as many as 12,000 ascetic monks, acclaimed as one of the greatest temples of its time. Walk among its *stupas*, holy caves and Buddha statues and you will see inscriptions carved into stone celebrating those that achieved enlightenment here, in silence and solitude, painting the ceilings of their hermitages with bright frescoes that can still be seen today. Climb the staircase, hewn directly from the rock, as pilgrims have done for centuries, and the entire park unfurls in waves of rolling green to the sea. Ancient *dagobas*, draped in jungle, poking through the canopy like whispers from a lost world.

That's Yala's secret: this is a jungle of enlightenment, the natural world sanctified with the quiet contemplation of 2,000 years – wild but elegant too, fierce but filled with style, just like the leopard itself.

WHERE: Southern Sri Lanka, 160 miles south-east of Colombo. The nearest town is Kataragama: *www.yalasrilanka.lk*

DON'T MISS: Time your visit with the annual Kataragama Festival, held in Kataragama town each summer. This huge religious celebration, attended by followers of Hinduism and Buddhism alike, features elephant parades, music, drumming and some of the most intense acts of devotion in the world – including hanging from hooks, rolling semi-naked in hot sands and traditional fire-walkers, who prove their faith by walking barefoot across a path of red-hot embers: *www.kataragama.org/kataragama-puja.htm*

TOP TIP: The best time for a leopard safari is May to the end of August, when visibility is better and animals congregate around watering holes. The park is closed annually from 1 September to 15 October.

WHILE YOU'RE THERE: Combine your visit with a stop at Minneriya National Park for the annual elephant gathering, the largest Asian elephant gathering on the planet, when hundreds converge on the banks of Minneriya reservoir to stave off the end of the dry season, from July to October – one of Sri Lanka's most spectacular wildlife events: *www.srilanka.travel*

ALTAI TAVAN BOGD NATIONAL PARK, MONGOLIA

Mongolia is Genghis Khan country. Born into humble origins – his father was poisoned before he was ten years old and his mother abandoned by the tribe – Chinggis, as he was known, the 'Universal Ruler', nonetheless rose to become the greatest conqueror the world has ever seen. In the 65 short years of his life, he united the warring tribes of the Mongolian steppe, some 1 million people, built one of the most feared armies in history and captured huge swathes of modern-day Russia, China, India and the Middle East – taking more than twice as much land as any other ruler on Earth, at any time, and connecting Eastern and Western civilisations for the first time in the process.

Today, his legend lives on. The Mongolians call their country 'The Land of the Blue Sky': there is a sense of limitless space here, of remoteness and vast emptiness, that even the stars cannot contain. There are many highlights: the plains of the Gobi Desert, the cultural richness of Ulaanbaatar, the spectacular ruins of Karakorum. But to truly experience the land of Chinggis, you must leave the city and roads behind and ride out into the wilds of the uncharted country where the people still follow the traditions of the old ways. You must come to Altai Tavan Bogd National Park.

Meaning 'five saints', for the five sacred mountains housed within the park, Altai Tavan Bogd stretches more than 2,000 square miles across the western edge of Mongolia, an immense expanse of 12,000-foot-high mountains, punctuated by thick glacier tongues, endless grasslands and emerald lakes with jagged peaks rising snow-capped and rugged all around. The trekking, especially on horseback (this being Mongolia, everything is better on a horse), is superb; the wildlife too: lynx, brown bear and even the endangered snow leopard hide out among these rocky crags and frost-bitten forests. But it's the space that gets you. The locals say it sets your *hiimori*, your 'wind horse', free and that's exactly how it feels: as unbounded as the breeze, a place for the spirit to soar.

There is fascinating history too. Hundreds of 'stone men', standing stones sculpted centuries ago, dot the landscape with intricately carved faces, long and stout, like the Mongolians themselves. But most impressive are the petroglyphs – about 10,000 in all, found at Tsagaan Salaa, near the base of the sacred Shiveet Hairhan Mountain, which is still worshipped by local tribes today. These ancient rock carvings are the most complete, and best preserved, visual record of the human history of the region – dating back as far as 12,000 years: men on horseback with spears and arrows, reindeers and ibex running scared, horns arching along their backs.

But even more spectacular is the living culture of Altai Tavan Bogd today. Two groups make their home here, the Kazakhs and the Tuva, both of whom still live a traditional nomadic way of life – herding livestock, moving with the seasons, sleeping in *gers*, or yurts (circular tents made of felt and hides), and offering almost unrivalled hospitality to their guests: all visitors are sacred – even the last morsel of food will be shared.

The Tuva, of which there are estimated to be only 3,000 left in the country, occupy the Tsagaan Gol Valley and are famous for their music. Throat singing, a kind of low, guttural chanting, is one of the oldest forms of singing in the world and the Tuvan are masters of it, training from childhood in order to be able to turn the folds of their throat into a kind of reverberation chamber that can produce multiple notes at the same time. The result is astonishing, almost otherworldly – entire resonant harmonies emitting from a single voice. But for the Tuvan it is merely a reflection of their beliefs, that all parts of nature have a spirit. The sounds they produce are reflections of the natural world around them, the animals, streams and harsh winds of the endless Mongolian steppe.

The Kazakhs are the largest ethnic population in the region, proud equestrians and archers, generous and warm, quick to share a drop of *airag*, fermented mare's milk – their wincingly strong home-brewed liquor, with any willing guest. These are the famous golden eagle hunters – the only community in the world to hunt with these magnificent birds. The eagles are not bred in captivity, but taken from nests at about four years of age – old enough to have learnt how to hunt from their mothers, but young enough to train. They spend years living with the family, being fed by hand and treated much the same as a beloved pet. In winter, they take them hunting, trekking on horseback, often for days at a time, until a fox, or other small mammal, is flushed into the open and the eagle is released to make the kill. But they are not worked to death. After a number of years of service, on a spring morning, the hunter releases the golden eagle one last time, leaving a butchered sheep on the mountain as a parting gift, returning the bird to the wild in order to ensure that there are new born chicks for future generations of Kazakh hunters to use.

That's what makes it beautiful here. This is not a dying art, not a museum piece. Traditional Mongolian culture is as strong today as it was almost a thousand years ago, when hordes of horseback warriors charged across the world. The Land of the Blue Sky is as limitless as it ever was, still unconquered, still fierce, contained by nothing but the stars above. Chinggis would have been proud of the country he forged and the people who still watch over it today.

WHERE: Western Mongolia. The nearest main town is Ulgii, which has regular flights from the capital Ulaanbaatar: *www.visitmongolia.com*

DON'T MISS: The Golden Eagle Festival, in Bayan-Ulgii, the same province as the park: two days of spectacular rural Mongolian culture featuring Kazakh hunters from all over the region competing in tests of speed, agility and accuracy

Photo: Altaihunters

as well as numerous performances of traditional dancing, singing and more. One of the greatest cultural festivals of the world and a highlight of any trip to Mongolia: *www.discover-bayanolgii.com/golden-eagle-festival*

TOP TIP: Make sure to spend at least one night, or more, in a traditional *ger* – a true taste of rural Mongolian life and a rare insight into one of the world's most fascinating traditional cultures. Most tour agencies will include at least one such night, many base their entire itineraries around such encounters. There are numerous operators: Nomadic Journeys is one of the oldest and most respected: *www.nomadicjourneys.com*

WHILE YOU'RE THERE: Visit Khustain Nuruu National Park, also known as Hustai National Park, just 60 miles west of Ulaanbaatar, Mongolia's buzzing capital city and gateway into the country. Home of Mongolia's treasured wild horses, the Przewalski or 'Takhi' as they're known, as well as a host of other wildlife, this is an excellent day trip or overnight excursion, which can be easily combined with the cultural sights of the city: *www.visitmongolia.com*

TUSHETI NATIONAL PARK, GEORGIA

Tusheti is the most spectacular national park you've never heard of. Hidden deep in the Caucasus Mountains of Georgia, right on the border of the Russian republics of Dagestan in the east and Chechnya in the north, these high passes of rugged peaks and traditional pastoral villages have been all but forgotten by time. Until 1975, there was no road access. Even today, it is completely cut off for most of the year, thick winter snows making access impossible, and even in summer the road to get here is regarded as one of the most dangerous in the world: 65 miles of precarious dirt paths with sheer 1,000-foot drops and no safety barriers.

But it's worth the sweat. To call Tusheti a lost paradise is, perhaps, too strong: life is hard, with few modern conveniences and long, cold winters. But it is, nonetheless, an incredibly joyful place, one deeply connected to the land around it, where the welcomes are warm and boozy and the folk music plays all night long.

The landscape is almost surreal in scale. Limestone ridges punch through the highlands like jagged spears, enormous glaciers reaching down in thick rivers of serrated grey ice, slopes plummeting thousands of feet to narrow gorges below, as if cut by a giant's axe. Colour is everywhere: in summer, the mountains are verdant green, awash with wildflowers, bright yellow sunbeams bursting through storm clouds above. This is the true high country, it feels different: lifted above the safety of the lowlands, more like soaring above the views than just seeing them with your eyes, everything is open, light and free.

The trekking, and horse-back riding, is sublime, following ancient shepherd paths along pristine, rolling summits, views unfolding beneath you in waves, too vivid to be real. But the soul of the park is the Tush people themselves. These semi-nomadic herdsmen spend summers up here, shepherding tens of thousands of sheep and cattle to the lower pastures when the first winds of autumn come. It's a time for celebration, when the people reconnect with their ancestral lands, ride horses, pick berries, feast and dance long into the night. Come, and you will be part of that celebration too.

Photo: Lidia Ilona

The largest village is Omalo, the capital of the region, but still just a handful of dirt roads and stone homes, absolutely nothing touristy or commercial, not even a shop. Above the village, on a spectacular rocky promontory, is the 13th-century ruined fortress of Keselo, one of the largest of dozens of medieval defensive towers, which are scattered across the countryside, used centuries ago to hide from invading armies. Gorgulta is smaller, but perhaps the most picturesque, set high on a rocky hilltop with incredible panoramic views across the entire park. While nearby Dartlo has some of the best-preserved architecture in the region; traditional dry-stone buildings, watchtowers, like castle turrets, and stone shrines, called *nishi*, where rams are still sacrificed to this day, their blood painted on the shrine walls for luck.

Days are spent trekking between these historic settlements, built on the edge of steep gorges like precarious fortresses in the clouds, or helping out with the chores of the village, milking cows, making butter or *dambal khacho* cheese, a local delicacy for which the Tush are famous. Nights are for celebration: drinking *chacha*, the local firewater, from out of ram horns, listening to the sweet melancholy of Tush folk singing, accordions and dancing, toasting Georgia, life, new friends and the promise of more *chacha* to come.

That's what makes Tusheti National Park one of the greatest in the world. Up here, surrounded by these small, tight-knit communities who welcome you as an old friend, it really does feel like you've discovered a place that time has forgotten – the simple joys of food and song, an ancient way of life clinging to the mountain tops, while the modern one, those lists and cares we know too well, goes on somewhere down there, out of reach, in the valleys far below. You may never have heard of it before, but come once and you'll never forget it again.

WHERE: North-east Georgia, about 175 miles north of the capital Tbilisi. The largest village of the region is Omalo: *www.tusheti.ge*

DON'T MISS: Time your visit with the Tushetoba Festival, held each summer in the region – a huge celebration of authentic Tushetian culture, with horse racing, cheese-making, traditional arts and crafts, music, dancing and more. The best way to experience the legendary hospitality of the Tush people: *www.georgiaabout.com/2013/07/17/tushetoba-festival-tusheti*

TOP TIP: Don't attempt to drive the Abano Pass road on your own. Incredibly narrow, at times barely wide enough to fit a single car, with precipitous drops and often icy conditions, an expert driver with a good 4x4 car is highly recommended. Check website for drivers, guides and help with booking accommodation in the park: *www.tusheti.ge*

WHILE YOU'RE THERE: Hike part of the new 1,000-mile Transcaucasian Trail, one of the most ambitious sustainable tourism projects of recent years, which links together rural communities across the Caucasus Mountains of Georgia, Armenia and Azerbaijan. Passing directly through Tusheti National Park, the new trail aims to provide much-needed resources to villages along the way, while helping to preserve the cultural heritage of this spectacular region at the same time. Find out more here: *www.transcaucasiantrail.org*

OCEANIA

RAPA NUI NATIONAL PARK, CHILE

In 1872, the French sailor and artist, Pierre Loti, arrived on Easter Island and wrote this in his dairy: 'In the middle of the Great Ocean, in a region where no one ever passes, there is a mysterious and isolated island; there is no land in the vicinity and, for more than eight hundred leagues in all directions, empty and moving vastness surrounds it. It is planted with tall, monstrous statues, the work of some now vanished race, and its past remains an enigma.'

That island, referred to more commonly now by its indigenous name, Rapa Nui, is the most remote inhabited place on the planet. Its nearest neighbour, the equally diminutive Pitcairn Island where mutineers from the HMS Bounty famously hid in the mid-19th century, is 1,000 miles away. The nearest continent, South America's Chilean coast, is more than double that. But this speck of volcanic land, just fourteen miles long and seven miles wide, is home to one of the most extraordinary and mysterious works of monumental art that the world has ever seen: the Moais.

Perched along the edge of the sea, as if standing watch, are 887 monolithic statues carved by the original inhabitants of the island. Depicting disembodied heads and torsos, some with their bodies buried deep underground, others reaching 40 feet tall and weighing close to 75 tonnes, they remain as enigmatic today as when Loti first dropped anchor here almost 150 years ago. How did a primitive civilisation, cut off from the rest of the world, carve such intricate sculptures and then move them, often many miles over uneven ground, to their final resting places on the coast? Why did they do it in the first place? Speculation has ranged from long lost ancient civilisations to alien intervention, but the truth that's emerging is as remarkable as the people of Rapa Nui themselves.

It is thought the first inhabitants arrived here sometime between AD 800 and 1200, rowing hundreds of miles across the wild uncharted ocean in nothing more than simple wooden canoes. To them, the island became known as *Te Pito o te Henua*, The Navel of the World. Nothing existed but this sliver of rugged volcanic rock and the unfathomable enormity of the Pacific on all sides. Yet, somehow, they blossomed, developing complicated agriculture, music and art as well as the only known written language of the time ever found in Polynesia – a kind of heliographic script called Rongorongo, which is still being deciphered to this day.

They began carving the Moais almost immediately. Using only stone chisels, called *toki,* each sculpture was carved by hand from the volcanic stone of the island, then placed on top of *ahu* bases, a kind of ceremonial platform – many with a red stone *pukao* on its head, like a crown. Once in their final resting place, eye sockets were carved into their long faces using white coral for the iris and black obsidian for the pupils, now marking the Moai as a 'living face'. It would have taken five or six men working together over a year to create a single one.

Transporting them was even harder. Broken statues litter the ground everywhere – only a third of the total Moais created ever made it to their final destination – showing that they were probably transported upright and would

Photo: Jantoniow

occasionally fall en route. For years it was thought that tree logs were used as rollers, but Rapa Nui legends speak of the statues walking there themselves and it turns out the legends may be true. A recent study proved that by fastening ropes around the Moai they can be rocked from side to side while simultaneously being pulled from the front – like moving a refrigerator – creating a kind of wobbly walking motion that slowly inches them forward.

As to their purpose, no one really knows. The Moai face inwards from the coast, rather than gaze out to sea, suggesting they are watching over the people. It is thought that each one probably represents the spirits of deceased chiefs or other important ancestors from the tribe. The word Moai means 'so that he can exist'. Their hope in building them may have been to somehow grant their leaders a kind of eternal life, to transfer their living energy into stone so that they could continue to protect the people.

Today, Rapa Nui National Park fulfils much the same role, guarding the Moais and preserving the island itself. Three of the best sites are Ahu Tongariki, the largest ceremonial platform in Polynesia, featuring fifteen well-preserved Moais; Anakena Beach, a perfect strip of white stand, backed by seven restored Moai; and the volcano Rano Raraku, where they were originally quarried and many half-finished pieces can still be found.

But a surprising highlight is the Orongo ceremonial village, which harks back to a completely different and unique part of the island's history: the birdman contest. In the 18th and 19th centuries, after contact had already been made with the rest of the world, an island-wide religion linked to the fertility god Makemake took root. Each year the islanders would gather on a narrow ridge, near the Orongo village, 1,000 feet above the ocean, for the birdman contest –

possibly the most dangerous race in the history of the world. Contestants would have to climb down the sheer cliffs, often falling to their deaths in the process, then swim through shark-infested water to the islet of Motu Nui 1,000 feet off shore, collect a fresh egg from the colony of birds nesting there and then return, scaling the cliffs and avoiding the sharks, without breaking the egg. The first to make it back was declared birdman for that year, and honoured with important status in the tribe.

Rapa Nui is a remarkable island. To be cast adrift in the middle of the southern seas, surrounded by the 'moving vastness' of the 'Great Ocean' as Loti described it, and yet manage to create one of the great artistic works of humankind is an incredible achievement. Their true purpose has, perhaps, now been finally realised too. The legend of the Moais has spread around the globe, continuing to protect the people of this island by helping to preserve their culture and heritage. Here, in Rapa Nui, the most isolated and remote national park on the planet, the spirit of the Moais lives on.

WHERE: Rapa Nui (Easter) Island, Polynesia, officially part of Chile. Fly from Santiago or Tahiti. The main town and gateway to the park is Hanga Roa:
www.parquenacionalrapanui.cl

DON'T MISS: The hike up to Ma'unga Terevaka, the island's high point at just over 1,500 feet, for spectacular views across Rapa Nui and the endless horizon of the ocean beyond – the best place for getting a true sense of just how remote you really are.

TOP TIP: Come the first two weeks in February (the heart of their summer) for the island's Tapati Rapa Nui festival, a colourful celebration of their indigenous culture and heritage including singing, dancing, canoe races and the Haka Pei – where competitors use a banana leaf to toboggan down the steepest hillside on the island: *www.imaginaisladepascua.com/ en/easter-islands/rapa-nui-culture/tapati-rapa-nui/*

WHILE YOU'RE THERE: There is, quite literally, nothing but ocean for more than 1,000 miles in all directions. However, most flights to Rapa Nui depart from Santiago, Chile. Plan to spend a few days exploring this vibrant capital as well as visiting the world-renowned wineries of the Colchagua Valley, nearby, before making the trip to Rapa Nui: *www.chile.travel/en*

FIORDLAND NATIONAL PARK, NEW ZEALAND

New Zealand was made for adventure. These two islands, in the middle of the Southern Pacific, are home to some of the boldest and most dramatic landscapes on the planet. From glaciers and snow-capped 12,000-foot peaks to volcanoes, hot springs and beaches as soft as silk: New Zealand is the world's playground. When Hollywood wanted to make a movie of J.R.R. Tolkien's masterpiece, *The Lord of the Rings*, there was only one place that was big enough to fit the bill. New Zealand is paradise on steroids, Eden with a dash of adrenaline thrown in. If you want to scream, sweat, gawp and laugh out loud then these two little islands are the place to be.

There are many excellent national parks here: the smoking red cones and emerald lakes of Tongariro, which doubles as Mordor in the film trilogy; the pancake rocks and lush forests of Paparoa; Abel Tasman's palm-fringed coast. But one place beats them all. Rising from the South Island, like a dragon arching its back from the depths of the sea, is Fiordland: a place of mist and dreams. At almost 5,000 square miles, this is the country's largest national park and its most breathtakingly beautiful too. Waterfalls cascade hundreds of feet into shimmering lakes, granite peaks poke through low clouds, covered in moss-dripped forests and through it all run the mighty fiords themselves, chiselled by glaciers, but they might as well have been carved by gods themselves, sculptors of Earth, wind and sea. There is power here; there is energy. You can feel it soak into your skin like steam.

The first to discover its beauty, of course, were the Maori, the indigenous people of New Zealand, fierce, proud warriors whose descendants still thrive in the country today. For them, it was indeed a divine land, cut by the *te hamo* axe, of the deity Tute Rakiwhanoa, a giant stonemason – how else could such a place exist, but by magic? They hunted red deer, caught trout from the rivers and gathered *pounamu* from the rivers, a translucent green stone, like jade, that they carved into powerful symbols worn by the spiritual leaders of the tribe.

Later, in 1773, the British explorer Captain James Cook arrived – the first European to lay eyes on the land. His notes and charts attracted sealers, whalers and prospectors. But, apart from a few small settlements, the land was too steep, too rugged and brash for them to stay. Fiordland was spared and, for the most part, it remains as untouched today as when Cook's ship first sailed in.

There are fourteen fiords in the national park. Doubtful Sound, the longest, is a haven for wildlife: fur seals and Fiordland crested penguins line the 26-mile winding

Photo: Sam Ferrara

shore; bottlenose dolphins and migrating whales fill the icy channels; and in the mountains, the flightless *takahē* bird, which was thought to be extinct until it was rediscovered in 1948. Nearby, Dusky Sound, where Cook first moored, is wild and remote, while further afield Doubtful Sound, 'the sound of silence', as it's known, is like the cloisters of some grand monastery.

But, perhaps, the most beautiful is Milford Sound, described by Rudyard Kipling as the 'eighth wonder of the world'. A staggering 26 feet of rainfall a year has grown an almost impossibly verdant landscape here: dense rainforest clings to the mountains like a thick green coat, giant cascades, taller than skyscrapers, plummet to the narrow bays, mist on the water, clouds low as fog, the dagger tip of Mitre Peak magnetising all eyes to its summit. The 19th-century explorer, James Hingston, wrote: 'For thousands of feet upwards the eye looks upon straight cut rocky frontages, not worn smooth by time, or by wind or water, but as sharply defined and as fresh looking, in all respects, as if riven asunder, but yesterday, by the stupendous wedges of Titanic Masons.'

Fiordland has that effect on you. Like the Maori before Hingston, and visitors ever since, there is something in the landscape here that drives us to evoke magic, something too dramatic, too perfectly composed, to be the mere result of geology and chance. New Zealand was made for adventure, but Fiordland National Park was made for something else too. There is inspiration here. It lifts you up. This is a land born from our imagination, as wild and limitless as if drawn from the pages of a fantasy book. Perhaps it was. Tolkien would have approved.

WHERE: South Island, New Zealand. The nearest town, and gateway to the national park, is Te Anau: *www.fiordland.org.nz*

DON'T MISS: The glow worm caves on the western shore of Lake Te Anau: thousands of tiny bioluminescent creatures light up the roof in sparks of iridescent colour, like looking at the stars (*www.teanau.net.nz/Glow-worm-caves*). Also, not to be missed is a scenic flight over the national park for incredible views, the best photographs and a unique perspective on the whole area.

TOP TIP: The kayaking and cruising throughout is excellent, some of the best in the world – especially on overnight trips, which moor up in remote bays, nothing but the gentle lap of the ocean all around. But the trekking, or 'tramping' as it's known here, is even better. Fiordland National Park is home to three of New Zealand's nine 'Great Walks', long-distance hut-to-hut hiking paths: the Kepler Track, the Routeburn Track and the Milford Track – all are widely considered to be some of the best hiking in the world, usually taking between three and five days to complete. Numbers are limited and reservations must be booked in advance:
www.newzealand.com

WHILE YOU'RE THERE: Visit Aoraki/Mount Cook National Park, 300 miles to the north, also on the South Island. Encompassing the highest peak in the country, known to the Maori as Aoraki – one of their most sacred spots – as well as spectacular glaciers, lakes and some of the best mountaineering in the southern hemisphere:
www.newzealand.com/int/national-parks/

ULURU-KATA TJUTA NATIONAL PARK, AUSTRALIA

Uluru was formed in the Dreamtime. In the eons before the universe began, ancestral beings rose up from the featureless void and manifested the world we see today. These spirits of the aboriginal people became birds and animals, travelling to the far reaches of the Earth to create mountains, deserts, rivers and forests. Once they had finished, once the world was created and had taken physical form, they transformed into it, becoming rocks and watering holes, the stars above. Not in myth or metaphor, but in actuality. For the aboriginal people of Australia, the land is spirit. There is no division between Earth and soul; all is sacred. But some places hold special significance. Uluru is more than just a rock. This is their great cathedral, the heart of the Dreaming, a symbol of the aboriginal people themselves.

Rising 1,141 feet from the surrounding desert plains, a great red monolith that glows bright pink with the setting sun, it is also one of the most spectacular geologic formations on Earth. Uluru, or Ayers Rock, as it's also known, is more than two miles long, a mile wide and extends a further one and a half miles under the ground. Ernest Giles, the first European to discover it, called it 'the remarkable pebble' – and so it is: a single stone, taller than the Eiffel Tower in Paris, or the Chrysler Building in New York City, embedded in the Earth as if placed there by supernatural powers.

Walk around this island mountain, as the ancestors of the aborigines have done for millennia, and you will find caves of prehistoric rock art, 5,000-year-old paintings of human faces, dancers and spirals, where sacred rituals are still performed and fresh paintings are still put to stone. You will see evidence of the Dreamtime, the aborigines say, in the formations of Uluru itself: the deep ridges on its side are tracks made by the carpet-snake people as they went to and from the water-hole, the depressions on top are where they rested; a green-tinted trail leading up to Lungkata's cave is the remnants of the lizard-man's scaly skin; a series of large holes above, his footprints as he scaled the cliff face to the summit above.

Nearby, still within the boundaries of the national park, are the Kata Tjuta mountains, also known as the Olgas; 36 ochre-coloured sandstone domes, the highest of which rises nearly 2,000 feet from the red desert. The great snake king Wanambi lives on the summit of their highest peak, the legends say, only coming down in the dry season. The hairs of his beard are the dark lines stained on the rock. His breath is the wind, which blows through the canyon. The pointed rocks in the East are the kangaroo man. Nearby, Mulumuru, the lizard woman, cradles her brother in her arms. The land is alive with stories. Come and you not only walk through a starkly beautiful landscape, ablaze with the fire colours of the desert, you walk through history too. You see the Dreaming come alive.

The aborigines' is the oldest living culture on Earth, they have walked these lands for the last 50,000 years. But what's truly remarkable is that their culture is still intact today. In other ancient cultures, we need historians to guess at the meanings of petroglyphs or how those people once lived, how they thought and what they believed. Here, we need only ask. There is a direct line to the past. The stories, songs and dances they perform today are the same ones since time immemorial, passed down from generation to generation in an unbroken line. The aborigines believe that by touching Uluru, they can touch the Dreamtime itself. Perhaps we can

Photo: Tong Li

touch something of that too, and remember what they've kept alive all these long years, what they teach us: that there is no division between Earth, body and spirit. That our soul is connected to the land. That it is all one.

WHERE: Two hundred and ninety miles south-west of Alice Springs. The nearest town is Yulara: *www.parksaustralia.gov.au/uluru*

DON'T MISS: The Talinguru Nyakunytjaku observation area, which looks out across both Uluru and Kata Tjuta – the best place to watch the sunrise and sunset, when the stones light up in bright hues of orange, red and amber.

TOP TIP: Hire a local aboriginal guide. Hearing their stories and history first hand is the only way to appreciate the true wonder of these incredible sites. Stop by the cultural centre to find out more: *www.parksaustralia.gov.au/uluru/do/cultural-centre.html*

WHILE YOU'RE THERE: It's not close to Uluru, nothing is, but a flight up to Kakadu National Park, 1,200 miles to the north, near Darwin, makes an ideal accompaniment to this trip. Deeply connected to aboriginal culture, but less well known, the park protects one of the largest rock art sites in the world, paintings up to 20,000 years old that tell the story of aboriginal life. There's also excellent hiking, wildlife, boating, birding and more: *www.parksaustralia.gov.au/kakadu*